Spanish Women and the Colonial Wars of the 1890s

# SPANISH WOMEN
# and the COLONIAL WARS
# of the 1890s

D. J. WALKER

LOUISIANA STATE UNIVERSITY PRESS

BATON ROUGE

This publication was made possible in part by a grant from the Program for Cultural Cooperation between Spain's Ministry of Culture and United States Universities.

Published by Louisiana State University Press
Copyright © 2008 by Louisiana State University Press
All rights reserved
Manufactured in the United States of America
FIRST PRINTING

Designer: Barbara Neely Bourgoyne
Typefaces: Whitman, text; Footlight MT Light, display
Printer and binder: Thomson-Shore, Inc.

Library of Congress Cataloging-in-Publication Data

Walker, D. J.
  Spanish women and the colonial wars of the 1890s / D. J. Walker.
    p. cm.
  Includes bibliographical references and index.
  ISBN 978-0-8071-3298-2 (cloth : alk. paper) — ISBN 978-0-8071-3316-3 (pbk. : alk. paper)
  1. Spain—History—Alfonso XIII, 1886–1931. 2. Spanish-American war, 1898—Women—
Spain. 3. Spanish-American war, 1898—Protest movements—Spain. 4. Women—Spain—
Political activity. 5. Women—Spain—Social conditions—19th century. I. Title.
  DP245.W35 2007
  973.8'90820946—dc22

                                                                        2007025212

The paper in this book meets the guidelines for permanence and durability of the
Committee on Production Guidelines for Book Longevity of the Council on Library
Resources. ♾

To Jack and Rosalie

# Contents

*Illustrations follow page 58*

# Acknowledgments

I am grateful to the staff of the Hemeroteca Municipal in Madrid. Working there over the years has been a genuine pleasure. Moreover, the services provided by this institution have proved indispensable for a scholar based outside of Spain. Alisa A. Plant, at the Louisiana State University Press, demonstrated exemplary promptness and care in guiding me through the publication process, and I thank her for her professionalism and courtesy. John T. O'Connor patiently read and reread this study. As always, his encouragement and expertise have been invaluable.

Above all, I have been inspired by the lives of the anarchist women whose work I refer to in this study. In their steadfastness and personal courage they are one of the finest examples I know of dedication to goals such as female literacy, living wages, and equal pay for equal work in the face of seemingly insurmountable scorn and hostility.

# Introduction

The sorrows of Mary [become visible] on the heights of Calvary, where all the horrors that a mother may experience here in this life pierce her heart. In order to understand those sorrows we need only recall the clear ministry that nature and Providence, acting in mutual accord, have assigned to mothers. Only a mother's love could transcend the pain caused by the gestation, birth, and rearing of her children. For this reason God has imbued maternity with overpowering propensities to sacrifice—propensities that resemble a prolonged suicide and constitute a perpetual holocaust.

EMILIO CASTELAR

On August 1, 1896, in the midst of a war against Cuban insurrectionists that had sparked scant public opposition, women in Zaragoza and subsequently in Chiva (Valencia) and Viso del Alcor (near Sevilla) marched in demonstrations protesting the government's conscription policy. The terms of military service were laid out in article 3 of the Spanish Constitution. Every Spanish male was obliged to defend the fatherland with arms when called upon to do so by the law and to contribute in proportion to his income to the expenses of the state, the province, and the municipality. The law of *reclutamiento y reemplazo del ejército* was established on July 11, 1885, and modified on August 21, 1896. Article 172 of the law of August 21, 1896, permitted exemption from service on the península upon payment of fifteen hundred pesetas and exemption from service outside the peninsula upon payment of two thousand pesetas (Hernández Sandoica and Mancebo 1978, 364).

The average wage earned by a journeyman in predominantly agricultural Spain was 1.5 pesetas per day; urban workers generally earned 2 to 5 pesetas daily depending on their degree of specialization (Puell de la Villa 1996, 216, 221). Families with some means made significant sacrifices to insure their sons against the draft, so that if they drew a low number in the lottery they could pay the commutation fee. Purchase of substitutes was legal. The price varied, as the following newspaper advertisement in *El Imparcial* on January 22, 1896, shows: "A cheap and legal substitute wants to go to Cuba" (A Cuba desea ir sustituto barato y legal). The cost of hiring a substitute generally ranged from 500 to 1,250 pesetas. Volunteers also offered their services for variable fees.

While Great Britain had a volunteer national service in the nineteenth century, some European countries and the United States had conscription policies similar to Spain's. Until 1872, when commutation was abolished, France, like Spain, had military conscription by lot *(tirage)*. Replacements could be purchased for from five hundred to twenty-five hundred francs (Schwartz 2004). In about 1895 a workingman's total annual income was fifteen hundred francs (Weber 1986, 206). The Italian state required all males to serve in the military at age twenty-one. By 1900 those who could afford to pay two thousand lire served as volunteers for one year instead of three (Rochat 1973, 1875). This option was used extensively by the middle classes, "making nonsense of claims that universal military conscription was egalitarian" (Whittam 1977, 151). During the U.S. Civil War, the Confederacy eventually called upon white males from seventeen to fifty years of age in a draft whose inequities caused much disgruntlement and resistance. The conscription policy in the North allowed men to avoid service by paying the government a commutation fee of three hundred dollars (equal to a worker's annual wages) or by paying a substitute, which was a more costly option (Chambers 1991, 216–19). Among those who paid the commutation fee were Andrew Carnegie and Grover Cleveland.

The Spanish government collected an average of 40 million pesetas each year in commutation fees during the colonial wars, which partially explains its reluctance to accede to public opinion—supported by anarchists, socialists, republicans, and federalists—favoring the abolishment of exemptions based on the ability to pay.[1]

According to press reports, the women who marched in Zaragoza shouted, "Let the poor and the rich go!" For many contemporaries this cry appeared to question not only the inequity of conscription but also the legitimacy of the government that condoned it. Both contemporary and later accounts of the 1895–98 insurrections in Cuba and the Philippines have devoted some space to these demonstrations, noting that they spotlighted a policy almost universally conceded to be unjust and potentially disruptive though rarely contested publicly. The question that historians have then gone on to ask—Did the demonstrations serve to undermine the legitimacy of the monarchy or contribute significantly to the political objectives of the various opposition groups active at the time?—has been answered in the negative.[2]

This study examines the context and representation of the 1896 women's protests not in order to reconsider the extent of their impact on immediate policy decisions but rather in order to ask how the protestors, as *women*, were portrayed in the press, in letters, and in other writings by contemporaries. Why, in view of the small number of demonstrations and the participation of so few women, did these protests receive so much attention both in Spain and elsewhere? What did the irruption of protests conducted by women mean to the power structure and to the various groups making up the opposition in Spain? How were women who appeared in public in an attempt to influence government policy viewed in relation to institutions that conditioned their lives, such as education, religion, science, and the law? In the late nineteenth century, governments sought to muffle calls for change connected to either the status of women or that of the lower classes. To what extent does the history of Spanish women in the 1890s afford glimpses into those government efforts, especially during a time of war, when all such issues were exacerbated?

These questions reveal the indebtedness of the following study to the lines of inquiry suggested by Joan Scott in her 1987 essay "Re-writing History," in *Behind the Lines: Gender and the Two World Wars*. She wrote: "By examining women's history—female experience, actions, and expressions, as well as policies and legislation formulated for them—as a part of political history, and by asking how women's history figured in national and international politics, we gain new understanding of that politics. The question then becomes, not what was the impact of the wars on women, but what does the history of women reveal about the politics of war?" (Scott 1987, 30).

Clearly, the protests in 1896 were widely depicted as marking a departure from Spanish women's traditional stances in times of war. Only thirty-six years earlier, at the time of the African war (1859–60), the statesman and fourth president of the First Republic (in 1873), Emilio Castelar, had echoed one of the provisions of the *levée en masse* ordered by the Committee of Public Safety in France in 1793. That document mandated a state of total war, with clear instructions for the role women should play: "The young men shall go to battle; the married men shall forge arms and transport provisions; the women shall make tents and clothing and shall serve in the hospitals; the children shall turn old linen into lint; the aged shall betake themselves to the public places in order to arouse the courage of the warriors and preach the hatred of kings and the unity of the Republic" (Anderson 1908, 184–85). Castelar similarly spelled out the roles of women and children in wartime: "Weak womankind [should] make bandages and salves to heal the wounds of our martyrs, innocent children should lisp the inspiring names of our heroes of old."[3]

Castelar's conception of women's role in wartime certainly could not allow for the actions undertaken by some Spanish women only eight years later. Poor women demonstrated against the *quinta* (conscription) during the 1868–78 war against Cuban insurrectionists just as they did in 1896. Nonetheless, in conflicts that seriously threatened national autonomy or territorial integrity women were commonly believed to have stood firm as patriots and sacrificed their sons willingly. In the 1895–98 wars with Cuba and the Philippines women were expected to maintain their traditional willingness to sacrifice for the sake of the nation: Spanish women would rather weep at a husband's or a son's gravesite than blush for lack of patriotic fervor, wrote Rafael Gasset in an article for *El Imparcial* on April 1, 1898. The women of Zaragoza, in particular, were traditionally viewed as supreme patriots, making their protest in 1896 all the more incomprehensible. Finally, if, as some commentators alleged, the women had not themselves initiated their actions, there was cause for alarm in the notion that Spanish women were susceptible to the machinations of Protestant pastors or *filibusteros,* the proindependence agents most often cited as the likely puppeteers behind the protestors.

The protests troubled those Spaniards in the 1890s who were encouraged by the mainstream press to support without question purportedly consensual views on women's relationship to war, beginning in their own century with the War of Independence (1808–14). The Carlist Wars (1833–40, 1846–49, 1872–76) and the first war against insurrectionists in Cuba (1868–78), along with the more recent short-lived war in Melilla (1893), were assumed to have perpetuated that consensus.

Commonly accepted attitudes about women and war in the earlier period often found expression in national myths and in fiction. The penologist Concepción Arenal and the novelists Benito Pérez Galdós, Emilia Pardo Bazán, and Armando Palacio Valdés, among other well-known figures, contributed significantly to this national imagery. In the 1890s a wealth of speeches, plays, narratives, pamphlets, essays, and images in popular illustrated journals and the press reiterated traditional attitudes and, in some instances, provided new ways of considering how women related to war. What were the attitudes and concepts that provided the context for later views on Spanish women's relationship to war?

CHAPTER ONE

# Spanish Women and War, 1808–1898

Indeed, at the very time that the great international struggle was drawing its last breath, the Civil War [liberals against traditionalists] was uttering its first cries; from the majestic, shattered, bloodied breast of the struggle [against Napoleon] the other fight emerged as if born of it. Like Hercules, it began to commit atrocities from the cradle.

BENITO PÉREZ GALDÓS, *El equipaje del rey José*

## WOMEN IN THE WAR OF INDEPENDENCE

Personal involvement in war or local conflicts was so common in nineteenth-century Spain that from 1808 until 1876 no generation escaped more or less direct experience of war or armed uprisings during childhood and youth. In a nation of approximately fifteen million people approximately two hundred thousand died fighting in the Carlist Wars alone—nearly as many as those who were killed in action fighting for Union and Confederate forces in the U.S. Civil War (234,414). The U.S. population was, moreover, more than double the size of Spain's, some thirty-two million in 1860.[1] While certain areas of the country escaped actual fighting, many Spanish men, women, and children were nonetheless directly affected by the War of Independence and the Carlist conflicts.

In the 1890s the press often reminded Spaniards of the heroic role women had played in the War of Independence (1808–14). Until 1891 it was believed that the first of those national heroines, Manuela Malasaña, had died actively resisting the French during the uprising of May 2,

1808, in Madrid. An article in *La España Moderna* of 1891 belatedly provided an accurate account of her death.[2] In fact, the fifteen-year-old girl had been summarily shot in compliance with the order to shoot any Spaniard carrying a weapon. Malasaña, a seamstress, wore a pair of scissors at her waist as she returned home from her workplace and thus fell victim to the order. But some stories do not easily give way to less satisfying facts established subsequently. Manuela figures alongside women such as the Condesa de Bureta and Agustina de Aragón in the 1984 edition of the *Guía del Museo del Ejército* (Guide to the Army Museum [Madrid]), in the section dedicated to the Sala de Heroinas. The reader is informed that her portrait depicts the heroine of May 2, 1808, "who fought by her father's side against the French until she was killed" (luchó al lado de su padre contra los franceses hasta su muerte) (Fiestas 1984, 58). Emilia Pardo Bazán, the prolific novelist, short-story writer, critic, and journalist, evoked the events of May 2, 1808, along with the accurate, revised account of Malasaña's "martyrdom," in an article written in 1891 for *La España Moderna* and republished in *La Ilustración Artística* on April 27, 1896. While she acknowledged the revelation of Malasaña's passive victimization, Pardo Bazán insisted that in every *natural* war, that is, in every war fought to defeat an invader, women take part as soldiers and as heros. Spanish women, she continued, have traditionally taken the lead in a spirited opposition to invaders, often preceding men. They have goaded men to action, they have ministered to the wounded, they have loaded weapons, and, if no men were left to fire them, they have fired them as well.

Benito Pérez Galdós represented women in one of his historical novels about the War of Independence, *Zaragoza* (1874), much as Pardo Bazán portrayed them a generation later. He depicted women, for example, spurring hesitant men on to fight and firing cannons in place of men when necessary. But unlike Pardo Bazán, Galdós's narrator here and the narrator of the much later *Zumalacárregui* (1898) express an essentialist view according to which women are endowed with quite different traits from men's. In *Zaragoza* the suggestion is that women in war often acted in conformity with their "true" natures. The narrator further remarks that heroism is not solely found in the valiant: it is largely a question of the inspiration of the moment, which explains why it is sometimes found in women and in cowards (Pérez Galdós 1953, 191). In *Zumalacárregui*, a novel that deals with the first Carlist uprising, the narrator notes how the "true" nature of women may be put to novel ends. He attributes to women mean-spirited hatreds and outbursts of fury, traits that the Carlist general manipulates in order to fire the men up for battle. "Zumalacárregui's genius" writes the narrator, "understood this spring, not comprehended by many, in the mechanism of war and sought to elicit the ferocity of the male by releasing the base, contemptible emotions of the female" (El genio de Zumalacárregui veía este resorte, por muchos inapreciable, del mecanismo de la guerra, y quería producir la ferocidad del varón con las pasioncillas villanas de la hembra) (Pérez Galdós 1958c, 333).

In *Zaragoza* Galdós singled out Manuela Sancho for praise as one of the brave women of that city. The names, likenesses, and exploits of two heroines in particular, Manuela Sancho and Agustina de Aragón, who resisted the sieges of Zaragoza in 1808 and 1809, often appeared in the 1890s press. Spaniards normally viewed these heroines as women who did their duty for the fatherland and then quickly retreated to their proper sphere. Outside of Spain as early as 1845 the North American feminist Margaret Fuller saw Agustina, the "maid of Saragossa," not only as a model of valor but as an example of the alternative choices open to women. In her study *Women in the Nineteenth Century* (1845) Fuller posed the question, "What will women do when they are free?" She answered that she did not know, "but if you ask me what offices they may fill; I reply—any. I do not care what case you put; let them be sea-captains, if you will. I do not doubt there are women well fitted for such an office, and, if so, I should be glad to see them in it, as to welcome the maid of Saragossa, or the maid of Missolonghi, or the Suliote heroine, or Emily Plater" (Fuller 1980, 159). Nineteenth-century Spanish commentaries on the actions of the women warriors whom Fuller mentions do not speculate on how female valor might find expression in other areas of life. For Spaniards these women are always exceptional, and they are strictly ad hoc armed defenders of the fatherland.[3]

Farther back in Spanish history, the seventeenth-century Catalina de Erauso, known as the Lieutenant Nun (Monja Alférez) because as a young novice she abandoned the convent and went on to pursue a new life in military service to the Crown, provided another, far more ambiguous example of a Spanish woman who had engaged in battle. The fact that Catalina dressed as a man, managing to conceal her sex for years, and fought, not against invaders of Spanish soil, but against the *indios* in America, did not diminish her fascination or prestige for nineteenth-century Spaniards. Joaquín María de Ferrer published the first edition of her *Vida (Historia de la monja Alférez doña Catalina de Erauso, escrita por ella misma)* in 1829.[4] In the 1870s, during the first Cuban insurrection, Juan Pérez de Montalbán's 1626 play about Catalina—written when she was still alive—was revived in one of Spain's principal theaters, and it was said to have been greatly applauded.[5] On November 24, 1875, Carlos Coello's three-act zarzuela *La monja alférez* debuted at the Teatro Jovellanos (known also as the Teatro de la Zarzuela) in Madrid. In his prologue to the published version of the zarzuela, José Gómez de Arteche, of the Academy of History, pointed out that Catalina's life raised very grave issues. This woman, he wrote, raised in a convent, metamorphosed into a soldier when she crossed the ocean—a soldier who was, moreover, a gambler, a ruffian, and a "gallant" in pursuit of every beautiful woman who crossed her always bloody path. Gómez de Arteche did not mention that after her retirement from military service Catalina flourished as a mule driver and perhaps a slave trader in Mexico. He granted that not a few women in Spain had concealed their sex in order to act with greater freedom on their exalted religious or patriotic sentiments. But there was a difference, he wrote, between the Varona de Villañañe, contending against the Batallador de Aragón, and the various other women who had fought for Spain and Catalina, who was in fact a murderer (she killed, among others, her own brother in a duel) and a repugnant and unnatural female (Gómez de Arteche 1875, vii–viii). Gómez de Arteche believed that her only saving grace was that when she was examined by qualified matrons in Huamanga (Peru), her hymen was found to be intact.

The Varona de Villañañe, a precursor of Catalina's, was a fierce twelfth-century noblewoman who was rewarded by Alfonso VII for fighting and taking prisoner Alfonso el Batallador of Aragón (king of Aragón and Navarra, 1104–34). Unlike Catalina, she married eventually, and when her husband died, she retired to a convent. Her story, appropriately retold in the romantic period (1848), accorded with the version of her life presented in Lope de Vega's play *La varona castellana* (before 1604).[6] The influential nineteenth-century polymath Marcelino Menéndez Pelayo discussed Lope's portrayal of the Varona, noting that she was much like Catalina but less mannish. Like Catalina, she was a duelist and quick to fight, and again like Catalina, she pursued women *as a cover to conceal her sex*. Menéndez Pelayo did not consider the possibility that either virago was attracted to women, although he recognized the pleasure spectators took in misunderstandings occasioned by women's crossdressing in this play and in plays by Lope de Vega's seventeenth-century contemporary Tirso de Molina. Finally, Menéndez Pelayo writes that Lope's great understanding of the nature of females led him to depict the Varona as in love [with a man] and jealous, "and with that, the entire card-castle of her military valor collapses" (con lo cual se viene a tierra todo el castillo de sus valentías) (Hijos de J. Espesa 1929, 93).

Coello's 1875 play, set in America, misrepresents the Lieutenant Nun by portraying a Catalina secretly in love with a fellow soldier. When circumstances force her to fight a duel with him and she strikes a blow that puts him at the point of death, she reveals her sex for the first time: "love has made me a true woman" (el amor me hace mujer) (act 3, scene 5). Clearly, some people who were aware of Catalina's story were struck above all by the unusual and eventful life she had led. Others, like Gómez de Arteche, perceived anomalies and paradoxes in holding her up as a model for emulation.

But for most people what the historian saw as Catalina's deeply flawed and "perverse" nature posed no problem. Among them was the professed antifeminist Eva Canel, who worked as a journalist and pro-Spanish publicist in Cuba during the 1895–98 insurrection. Canel liked to refer to herself, and to have others refer to her, as another Monja Alférez. Photographs reveal that both inside and outside Cuba Canel usually wore the constraining, thoroughly feminine garments prescribed for women in her time but that on occasion she donned the military-style blouses and skirts modified for women that some Spanish women in Cuba affected (Simón Palmer 1992, 299). Neither she nor any other Spanish woman, so far as is known, engaged directly in battle against the insurrectionists. Nonetheless, her unlimited support for General Weyler's reconcentration policy, along with her tireless efforts to combat independence for Cuba, paralleled Catalina's service in behalf of the empire and no doubt motivated Canel's appropriation of the earlier heroine's appellation. In another striking parallel, Catalina de Erauso was rewarded in later life by Philip IV, who granted her a soldier's pension, and by Pope Urban VIII, who granted her a dispensation to continue dressing as a man. Canel was rewarded in later life, not by the king, but by the dictator Primo de Rivera, who made her a member of the Order of Isabel la Católica and subsequently awarded her the Medalla de Oro de Ultramar. In 1921 Pope Benedict XV bestowed upon her the Croce Pro Ecclesia et Pontifice.[7]

On August 31, 1896, one month after the women in Zaragoza demonstrated, a columnist for *El Imparcial* alluded to their march as that "minor, passing nuisance" (leve y pasajero disgustillo) and wrote that not long after the demonstration a young woman determined to follow her husband to Cuba had disguised herself as a soldier and was on a train heading for the port of embarkation when she was discovered. The columnist seized the opportunity to trot out some of the principal heroines reviewed above in a reassuring paean of praise to the innate patriotism of the Spanish woman: "[The woman's] cap fell off; her abundant hair was revealed, and she could not then pull off the heroic deception that immortalized Catalina de Erauso. The lineage of the Monja Alférez never dies out! The race epitomized by the artillery maids Manuela Sancho and Agustina de Aragón is neither exhausted nor does it fade away!" (¡Cayósele entonces la gorra; se le vio la abundosa cabellera, y no pudo lograrsele la heroica superchería que inmortalizó a doña Catalina de Eraso [sic]! ¡Casta que no se apura ni se agota, ésta de Manuela Sancho y Agustina Aragón, las Artilleras!).

One year earlier Kasabal (José Gutiérrez Abascal), in his column "Madrid," had struck the same note of praise for Spanish women's patriotism:

Woman has always been the support, the guiding spirit, and even the companion of the soldier in our land. With her encouragement she has inspired him to persevere in all our conflicts, and if our civil wars have been so hard fought, it is due to the part women have played in them. During the War of Independence there was not a single mother who, though it tore her heart out, wished to keep her son at home, and all mothers encouraged their sons to fight on behalf of the country. During the siege of Zaragoza, when there were not enough men to fire the cannons, women fired them, and when heroic deeds are recounted, Agustina Aragón and the Countess of Bureta will never be forgotten.

Women, weak and timid in the course of ordinary life, are transformed in supreme moments and perform the greatest acts of heroism.[8]

This view of Spanish women regarding their willingness to fight and to sacrifice their sons for the good of Spain would prevail throughout the nineteenth century. Only occasional acts and discrepant opinions would suggest to the public that its validity might be questioned.

Fictional Spanish women engaged in battle figure in two Spanish plays, *Cuba libre* (1887) and *Cuba* (1896). *Cuba libre,* by Federico Jaques y Aguado and Manuel Fernández Caballero, presents a Spanish woman who with her husband has lived in Cuba for many years and is fighting on behalf of the insurgents. Indeed, she heads a band of *amazonas,* who at one point boast about using their feminine wiles to weaken and conquer the male enemy. Not only is the Spanish woman a turncoat but she wears the pants in the family—a clear sign that she has overstepped the bounds of acceptable female behavior. She sees the error of her affiliation with the insurgents when a mulatto asks for her daughter's hand in marriage: "What an atrocity! A mulatto marry Cachita!" The mulatto answers, "Why not? There are no colors in Free Cuba" (¡Qué atrocidad! ¡Con Cachita casarse un mulato! ¡Y por qué no! ¡En Cuba libre no hay colores!) (67). The mulatto threatens to hang the woman and her husband if they do not consent to the union, but the situation is saved by a relative who loves the daughter and is fighting on behalf of Spain.

*Cuba,* by Jesús López Gómez, presents a Spanish woman fighting alongside Spanish soldiers, who refer to her as "the heroic Amazon who is to lead us to victory" (la heroica amazona que ha de conducirnos a la victoria) (28–29). When her husband expresses surprise at seeing her in pursuit of the enemy, she explains, "Women become virile when they see their men lying dead" (Son mujeres varoniles al ver al que adoran muertos). Women fighting for Spain are not represented as unfeminine in *Cuba*.

I have found no reports in the Spanish press on Spanish women combatants in Cuba or in the Philippines. There apparently was interest in reports of female insurrectionist combatants in the Philippines and in Cuba, but, apart from drawings or photographs of armed Cuban women that appeared occasionally in the Spanish illustrated press, there was little else of substance on their activities. On September 22, 1895, *El Imparcial* reported the capture in Placetas of a black woman, Jacoba Zulueta, who had fought dressed as a man and who, the report noted, had shown great courage in battle. The humorist Luis Taboada, on the other hand, penned a mocking account for *El Imparcial* on May 15, 1896, of the death in battle of a *mambisa* (female rebel). He wrote that Sra. Álvarez, head of a battalion of *amazonas*, had fought until Spaniards wielding machetes cut her into "albóndigas" (little meatballs). In 1896 General Weyler told the American reporter Kate Masterson that the women fighting Spaniards in Cuba, mulattoes for the most part, were fiercer than men.[9]

Several women fought alongside men in the Philippines, including Josephine Bracken, the wife of the Filipino separatist José Rizal. Accompanied by two of Rizal's sisters, Josephine chose to fight after her husband's execution (Reverter Delmas 1897, 523). Rizal's sister Josefa was the first president of the women's unit of the Katipunan, the underground insurrectionist movement, and a Mason (Soriano 1995a, 100–101). Agueda Kahabagan, known as Henerala Agueda, was said to enter the field of battle dressed in white, armed with a rifle and a bolo. She was listed as the only woman among the generals in the Army of the Filipino Republic, an appointment she received in 1899 (Reyes Churchill 1995, 66). The fortnightly journal *La Política de España en Filipinas* reported on December 31, 1896, that a group of women had participated in the battle of Binakayan in Kawit. According to the Spanish account, the women rebels taken by the Spaniards "knelt down and allegedly even asked for forgiveness from the Spanish soldiers who attacked the Filipino trench. However, it was reported that when a Spanish soldier turned away his gaze on them, the two Filipino women forthwith got out their sharp bolos surreptitiously hidden in their long skirts and lunged toward the soldier. The other Spanish soldier [sic] however noticed this move and immediately fired their Mauser rifles on the hapless women" (qtd. in the English paraphrase of Medina 1995, 88–89).

Gregoria Montoya y Patricio was a casualty of an earlier battle. In November 1896 she died, struck down by a cannonball while leading a unit of thirty men. Her death illustrates the power that the religion inculcated by the Spanish clergy wielded over the vulnerable, less educated women in the Philippines. She "climbed atop the fort and stood there, bravely shouting and waving a white piece of cloth. This cloth, they said, was a cover for the chalice used by a priest in singing mass, and the poor woman waved it as a charm to ward off bullets. But contrary to other hopes, she hurtled and dropped dead to the ground after being hit instantly" (Medina 1995, 89). Like many other women who have chosen to fight in defense of whatever cause, Gregoria reportedly fought above all to avenge her husband's death in battle. While the women named here—with the exception of Josephine Bracken—were not known in Spain during the Philippine insurrection, they were celebrated heroines and martyrs in their homeland.

It is worth noting that the influence of Spanish priests over rebel women both in the Philippines and in Cuba posed a significant problem for insurgents. José Rizal wanted to sever the bonds between women and priests because he did not trust the priests to maintain the secrecy of the confessional. One Spanish observer asserted that almost all the separatist conspiracies had been denounced to priests by indigenous women devoted to Spain (O'Connor 2001, 67). Teresa Prados-Torreira (2005, 45) writes that in Cuba in 1851 Josefa de Agüero allegedly confessed to a priest that her husband, Joaquín de Agüero, along with co-conspirators hiding in the mountains near Camagüey, was plotting to overthrow Spanish rule. The priest supposedly informed the Spanish authorities, and in due time Josefa's husband was executed. Prados-

Torreira notes that whether this account was accurate or not, in the minds of the rebels the Catholic Church was not on the side of Cuban patriots and was not to be trusted.

### THE CARLIST WARS

Only nineteen years after the French were expelled from the peninsula, what had begun as a dynastic dispute over Fernando VII's rightful heir escalated into a series of armed conflicts, the Carlist Wars. Women performed the same kinds of support work in these fratricidal wars that their forebears had performed in earlier wars. On occasion, women participated in the fighting as they had done in the War of Independence. In March 1838, for example, the traditional combative patriotism of the women of Zaragoza was on display as they fought the Carlist forces with stones, water, and boiling oil, thus contributing to the Carlists' defeat (Romeo Mateo 2000, 219). Nonetheless, no legendary warrior-heroines emerged from the Carlist Wars.[10] One of the most vivid stories to come out of these conflicts recounted the fate of a real woman, a passive victim, the mother of the Carlist general Cabrera, who was taken hostage and ordered shot by the liberals.

In Benito Pérez Galdós's historical novel *La campaña del Maestrazgo* (1958a), set in 1837 and written in the spring of 1899, a young soldier describes the circumstances surrounding the execution of Cabrera's mother and the anguish he felt because of the part he played in her death (he headed the firing squad). When he has finished his painful account, he asks,

> Why are we fighting? At bottom, I see no reason for all this carnage. Liberty! Religion! . . . We have more than enough of both! Don't you agree? . . . The Queen's rights, Don Carlos's rights! When I stop to think about the reasons for this war, I can't help but laugh . . . and I laugh and I think, and I end up convinced that we're all crazy. Do you believe that Cabrera cares about the rights of his male Majesty? And do these people here care about the rights of her female Majesty? I believe that men fight for domination, and that's all; for power, for the right to meddle in everything, for the chance to be the one to parcel out the

piece of bread, the handful of garbanzo beans and the half-glass of wine that comprise the patrimony of every Spaniard . . .

¿Por qué combatimos? Ahondando en el asunto, encuentro que no hay razón para esta carnicería. ¡La libertad, la religion!... ¡Si de una y otra tenemos dosis sobrada! ¿No le parece a usted?... ¡Los derechos de la reina, los de don Carlos! Cuando me pongo a desentrañar la filosofía de esta guerra, no puedo menos de echarme a reír..., y riéndome y pensando, acabo por convencerme de que todos estamos locos. ¿Cree usted que a Cabrera le importan algo los derechos de su majestad varón? ¿Y a los de acá los derechos de su majestad hembra? Creo que se lucha por la dominación, y nada más: por el mando, por el mangoneo, por ver quién repartee el pedazo de pan, el puñado de garbanzos y el medio vaso de vino que corresponden a cada español... (793)

Passive women victims of an unjustifiable war and the antiwar reflections their deaths provoke constitute one of the principal themes of *Cuadros de la guerra,* a collection of brief narratives published in 1883 by the eminent sociologist and penologist Concepción Arenal. Arenal based her opposition to war in general on religious and judicial principles. A spokesman for the narrator comments on the ruin, physical and moral, that he witnesses in an area devastated by the warring factions: "It is certain that war is an infraction of God's law, a mockery of His commandments, an attack against all laws, an abandonment of all duties: it honors what is monstrous, it sponsors what is vile, and there is no impiety that it does not sanction nor perversity that it does not justify."[11] Galdós ends his 1899 *episodio nacional* (historical novel) *Vergara,* set in 1837, with an account of an actual incident that illustrates the impiety and perversity Arenal found in all wars. One of the historical protagonists of this *episodio,* the Carlist general Maroto, was reviled as a traitor by die-hard supporters of the Carlist cause for his role in bringing about the compromise of Vergara, which temporarily ended the bloodshed between Carlists and Cristinos (supporters of María Cristina, queen regent). Galdós notes that the general's daughter, Margarita, sometime later went to confession, after which the priest asked her her name. When she replied timidly that it was Margarita

Maroto, the priest rose up in a fury and angrily sent her away, refusing to give her absolution (Pérez Galdós 1958b, 1068).

Arenal was thirteen years old when the first Carlist war began. Years later, in her capacity as a Red Cross observer, which involved visiting hospitals, she became a firsthand witness to some of the conflicts of the last Carlist war. Arenal's descriptions of incidents in the war have been compared to Goya's *Disasters of War* in the sense that the vignettes in which mothers, babies, or children figure contain images as striking in their depiction of cruelty and brutality and their consequences as those of Goya's etchings. In one such story a young woman has been forced to lead several enemy soldiers through her house in search of men the soldiers believe to be hiding there. Suddenly, when the young woman steps before a window she is shot by soldiers outside the house, who have been ordered to fire at anything that moves. The enemy patrol leaves her, and she crawls to the room where her infant lies. When she is found dead some hours later, the baby is folded in her arms upon her bloody breast, still trying to nurse.

Arenal was intent upon driving home one principle: that war, unless it is a defensive struggle waged against aggressors who seek to deprive a population of its natural rights, constitutes an attack on the laws of the land. She illustrates the rupturing of bonds that should normally hold a society together with a reference to a case that she found particularly despicable, that of a fourteen-year-old boy who was "seduced," that is, persuaded to sneak away from his family in order to volunteer, thereby making a mockery of paternal authority and family unity (1942, 132). Arenal also refers to acts customarily left unmentioned by other commentators on the war by alluding, for example, to one of the consequences of providing lodgings for soldiers, the rape of local women and girls (98). Arenal's vignettes depicting individual suffering, especially of women and children, similarly aim to demonstrate how moral bonds are destroyed in the course of an unjust war.

One of her stories describes the plight of an artillery detachment encamped above the town it means to shell. The men are desperate for water. A mother ill in her bed in the town sends her daughter off to fetch water for their small garden. The child takes pity on the thirsty soldiers she encounters outside the town. She not only gives them the jug of water she is carrying but returns for more. Before she leaves for home, she asks the soldiers to spare her house in the coming bombardment. The grateful men and their officer take note of the exact location of the house on the square where the girl's mother lies, too ill to move. The bombardment begins and is soon over. When the officer and his men enter the town, they recall their promise to the child. They locate the house but find that it has been shelled. Inside, the officer discovers the girl's body next to her mother's. The men contribute money for the child's white coffin wreathed in flowers, which they accompany to the cemetery.

Arenal's women (like General Cabrera's mother) are not victims in the same sense that Manuela Malasaña was. Malasaña was perceived to have died, not a victim, but a martyr in a just war and could therefore serve as inspiration for later generations even if (as was learned in 1891 and largely ignored) she had put up no active resistance to the French. The women and children in Arenal's stories are not victims of cruel invaders: they are victims of the lawlessness and moral confusion of civil war. In this sense their deaths may be interpreted much as modern viewers interpret the deaths of noncombatants in Goya's *Disasters of War*, as chaotic and senseless.

In 1881 Armando Palacio Valdés published *Marta y María*, a novel that brought him a large amount of money and considerable fame not only in Spain but in Europe as a whole and America. Set during the last Carlist war, it is the story of two sisters, one of whom, Marta, never questions her future role in life as wife and mother, while her sister María embodies some of the ambiguities implicit in the figure of the Monja Alférez, Catalina de Erauso. Near the end of the novel, the emotionally exalted María allies herself with a group of Carlists. She is prepared to join them; in addition to giving money for the cause, she is willing to fight alongside them. Her alarmed family thwarts her plan by removing her to a convent, where she is to reflect on her actions and reconsider her choices. Undaunted, María appears to welcome this decision since it may permit her to indulge the perverse inclinations already hinted at by the author. Palacio Valdés strongly implies that María derives erotic pleasure from having her young, attractive maid lash her while she kneels naked on the floor gazing at a figure of the crucified Christ.

From the point of view of his "liberal" contemporaries, Palacio Valdés's representation of María as a highly problematic Christian whose "mysticism" appears to be grounded in a perverse sexuality undoubtedly discredited her adherence to the Carlist cause.[12] Just as significantly, the portrayal of Maria's sister, Marta, as a model Spanish woman content to be a wife and mother discredited most activity outside the sphere of home and family, excepting charitable work, for women of the comfortable classes. Direct engagement in war, except in a just war of defense against invaders, and indirect participation in the form of political activity were implicitly deemed inappropriate for a normal, genuinely feminine woman.

Between July and September 1896—the period during which the women's demonstrations in Zaragoza and elsewhere were taking place—Miguel de Unamuno finished writing his novel on the last Carlist war, *Paz en la guerra* (Caudet 1999, 11n2). Within the context of that final conflict Unamuno relates the story of a young man who fought in the first Carlist war and later saw his only son volunteer to fight for the Carlist cause in 1873. The wife of the young man and mother of the volunteer provides a pristine version of the archetypal Spanish Christian woman. One of the principal ideas developed in the novel is the notion that wars are inevitable, that the hot blood of boys entering puberty impels them not only toward sex but also to acts of violence that find ready expression in war. Unamuno represents the role of women in this unending cycle of sex and death as one of resignation. The wife of the novel's young man sees him off to the first Carlist war urging him to comply with the will of his uncle (who stands in the place of his father) and the will of God as interpreted by priests. When their only son resolves to become a volunteer, she places a scapular around his neck, fastens a "deténte bala" (bullet stopper), a cloth pouch embroidered with the Sacred Heart of Jesus, to his chest, and, as he departs the family home, cries: "Don't leave a single liberal standing! War to the enemies of God! Don't come back until Don Carlos is king, and if they kill you, pray for me!" (¡No dejes un *guiri* para muestra! ¡Guerra a los enemigos de Dios! No vuelvas a casa hasta que sea rey don Carlos, y si te matan, reza por mí) (Unamuno 1999, 253).

Unamuno's fictional mother belongs to the merchant class. She and her husband do not depend on their son for support. He is, moreover, a volunteer, not a conscript. The son dies for the cause, and his parents live out the rest of their lives in quiet, Christian resignation. Mothers in the countryside, equally obedient to the counsel of their priests, cry out as some of their sons are taken away by press gangs: "For the sake of religion, go now, even though you go to your death" (¡Por la religión vete, aunque sea a morir!) (277). But the fathers, as they watch their sons depart, reflect with regret on the loss of "the strong arms that were leaving without finishing the work, before the threshing" (lo que sentían éstos eran los brazos que se les iban, sin acabar la faena, antes de la trilla) (277). Unlike other poor mothers, real or fictional, these poor mothers—at least until their husbands are also taken away by press gangs—put God's demands, as interpreted by priests sympathetic to Carlism, before their own economic interests.

### THE CUBAN INSURRECTION OF 1868–1878

Many Spaniards in the nineties were able to recall the protests mounted by poor women against the *quinta* (conscription) during the 1868–78 insurrection in Cuba. The government and the conservative press were alarmed at the threat to public order posed by demonstrations held in the winter of 1869, some of which were composed primarily of women. Albino Feijóo Gómez lists the "wave" of demonstrations that took place in Madrid, with 7,000 participants; Barcelona, Valladolid, Almería, and Orense, with 6,000; Talavera, with 3,000; Málaga, with 17,000; and Valls, with 6,500. He cites a poem read by one of the women in the Madrid demonstration that clearly stated the revolutionary temper of the protestors:

Let not Spaniards cry liberty
Let them not say that we have it in Spain
That it bears a flag of higher honors.
Each soldier drags a chain
and every mother seated before her hearth
mourns the loss of her most beloved son.
And in the tears her agony causes her to shed
she curses the tyranny of the law.
There is no liberty where a mother weeps
and watching her son grow, hopes
that a hand from heaven will cripple him.
Who is the law to bring death
to a woman of great spirit?
Who is the law to mark as a slave
the youth who completes twenty Aprils?
He who touches a creature raised free by a father
is surely not called the Law, but tyranny.[13]

Although the demonstrating women, it appears, were what drew attention to anti-*quinta* sentiment, the government cracked down, not on them, but on republicans believed to be controlling them.[14] Whether or not they were in fact controlled by republicans, it was true that the Republican Party made opposition to the *quinta* an important part of its platform. Raymond Carr (1982) notes that the *quinta* system "was used by the Republicans in the first attempt by any Spanish party to recruit women: the mother weeping for her lost sons was the Democratic reply to the image of the wife attentive to the confessor" (312). It is noteworthy that in her novel *La Tribuna* (1882), set in the late 1860s and early 1870s, Emilia Pardo Bazán remarked on the strange fact that the religious devotion of the *cigarreras* who worked in a Galician tobacco factory increased in intensity even as their adherence to the anti-Carlist, prorepublic cause became more fervent (1956, 156). The explanation for this seeming paradox may stem from the novelist's earlier speculation that women in general supported the First Republic because it promised an end to conscription (132).

While women who opposed inequitable conscription, and who may or may not have supported the First Republic, demonstrated against the *quinta,* others passively watched their sons embark for Cuba, while still others went to Cuba as Sisters of Charity, earning much praise in the press for their maternal selflessness and devotion. The Order of the Sisters of Charity, founded by St. Vincent de Paul (1575–1660), was dedicated to the teaching of the young and the care of the sick, the old, and the poor. The Concordat of 1851 stipulated that the Congregation of Sisters of Charity were to be paid for nursing the poor in public institutions.

The sisters' selfless activities in Cuba as nurses and teachers elicited admiration long before the insurrections of 1868 and 1895. During both conflicts Sisters of Charity manned the hospitals in Cuba and served on ships, caring for men going to and returning from the island. They were lauded frequently in the press, though it should be noted that admiration of the sisters was not universal either during the Cuban insurrections or subsequently. Santiago Ramón y Cajal, who spent weeks in a Cuban hospital staffed by the sisters during the first insurrection, later wrote that they seemed quite inured to the suffering of their patients.[15] Nonetheless, their ministrations inspired male poets to write lyrics extolling the capacity of women to sacrifice their own good for the common good. One such lyric, by José María Gabriel y Galán, is entitled "Las hermanas de la caridad en la Guerra." The poet reflects on how picayune men appear to him in comparison with the moral and spiritual grandeur of the sisters. The last four stanzas convey the essential message: war is the work of men in thrall to destructive urges, while women such as the Sisters of Charity, moved by compassion, may redeem the world:

> Who has thrust you,
> human angels,
> into the midst of the thunderous
> clamor of battles,
> where men
> fight and destroy themselves
> like lions?
>
> Who commands you,
> unfortunate women,
> to close the eyes

of those who die,
and to act as mothers
to those who far from their own mothers
shed their blood?

Who lifts you to the height
of heroism?
Who gives you strength
for martyrdom?
Who obliges you
to immolate your own life
for that of another?

I know the answer, o holy women:
Your heroism
is that of the loving
children of Christ.
There is no one who can deny it!
Christian charity
can accomplish anything![16]

The sisters also served as subjects for illustrators and painters. In 1897, during the second Cuban insurrection, Cecilio Pla presented a canvas entitled *Heroinas* to the Exposición de Bellas Artes in Madrid. The heroines, all young and attractive, were Sisters of Charity seated in a railway station awaiting transport to ships bound for Cuba. The novelist and art critic Jacinto Octavio Picón praised the painting in *El Imparcial* on May 7, 1897, in an article that explicitly approved of compositions depicting dramatic scenes or events related to war and its consequences.

When Clara Barton in her capacity as a Red Cross worker arrived in Havana on February 6, 1898, she went to Los Fosos, one of a complex of buildings filled with *reconcentrados*, people whom General Weyler had forcibly moved from their homes in the countryside, where they might aid the insurgents, to towns and cities. Her account of what she saw, including mention of the service provided by the Sisters of Charity, is quoted below at some length since accounts such as hers of the desperate plight of the *reconcentrados* were seldom published in Spanish newspapers at the time. It should be noted, however, that one of the correspondents for *El Imparcial,* Domingo Blanco, wrote "Algo sobre los reconcentrados" (Something about the *reconcentrados*) in a dispatch published on December 6, 1897, shortly after General Weyler, author of the *reconcentrado* policy was relieved of his command on October 9, 1897. Blanco began by comparing the wasted bodies of the *reconcentrados* to the soldiers returning from Cuba who were devastated by disease, thus suggesting that suffering was dealt out equally to Spanish soldiers and noncombatant rural Cubans. He then wrote that Weyler's policy had been entirely justified and that fewer people would have died of starvation if only they had possessed the will to work the "zonas de cultivo" established near the towns where they were confined. In Güines, he wrote, he had witnessed forty-five hundred *reconcentrados* cast out onto the streets or dying in wretched shacks. But in San Felipe the *reconcentrados* had had the "strength of will" to cultivate the parcels of land allotted to them.

It was clearly almost impossible for Spanish reporters to describe the plight of the *reconcentrados* to Spanish readers while the war was being waged. Nonetheless, while I have found few graphic references to the suffering of the *reconcentrados* in the Spanish press, Stephen Bonsal, an American reporter who later testified before the U.S. Senate Foreign Relations Committee on what he had seen in Cuba (with a view toward persuading the United States to recognize belligerency, thus compelling the combatants to conform to the rules of war), wrote in his book *The Real Condition of Cuba Today* (1897): "That noble paper, the *Imparcial,* of Madrid, has told the Spanish people of all the horrors and the cruelties that are being perpetrated in Cuba in their name. The whole infamy of Weyler's scheme of pacification has been exposed in eloquent and adequate language in the columns of this and other Spanish papers, which have refused to allow themselves to be blinded by the bull-baiting fury that is prevalent in Madrid today" (147).

In general, Spanish liberals saw the press as timid and reactionary in its coverage of the wars in Cuba and the Philippines. Conservatives perceived it as overly sympathetic to dissenters and too willing to criticize the government. The Duque de Tetuán, for example, an ex-minister of state and former member of a right-wing faction that had left President Mateo Práxedes Sagasta's ministry of 1885–90, asserted in reference to the period 1895–97 that the Spanish press, out of a misguided sense of professional duty to provide information, "constituted itself, in effect, as the official organ of the *filibusteros,* insurgents, and enemies of Spain" (se constituyó de hecho, en organismo oficioso y propagandista de los filibusteros, insurrectos y enemigos de España) (Fernández Almagro 1969, 441).

Clara Barton's grim account of what she saw in Los Fosos is lightened only by her description of the order and discipline imposed by the sisters in the house they managed:

> On landing, we resumed our carriage and drove to Los Fosos, a large, long building filled with reconcentrados,—over four hundred women and children in the most pitiable condition possible for human beings to be in, and live; and they did not live, for the death record counted them out a dozen or more every twenty-four hours, and the grim, terrible pile of rude black coffins that confronted one at the very doorway, told to each famishing applicant on her entrance what her exit was likely to be.
>
> We went from room to room, each filled to repletion—not a dozen *beds* in all. Some of the inmates could walk, as many could not,—lying on the floor in their filth—some mere skeletons; others swollen out of all human shape. Death-pallid mothers, lying with glazing eyes, and a famishing babe clutching at a milkless breast. Let me attempt no further description. The massacres of Armenia seemed merciful in comparison.
>
> We went our rounds, and sought the open air; drove to another building of like character, but in a little better condition—one hundred and fifty-six inmates. These persons had been recommended by someone, who paid a little for each, and thus kept them from daily starvation. From here to the third building (the Casino), of about an equal number, still a little better off.
>
> From here to the fourth building (La Yocabo)—two hundred and fifty persons, the best of the reconcentrados. The sisters of charity had recently taken hold of these, and cleanliness and order commenced to appear. The children had books, were being taught, and rooms were fitted out for some kind of industrial training. This place seemed like heaven in comparison).[17]

Most of the fictional and nonfictional representations of the Sisters of Charity focused on their maternal instinct and their spirit of self-sacrifice. A different aspect of their service was highlighted in an article by Domingo Blanco, the abovementioned correspondent in Cuba for *El Imparcial*, that appeared on December 18, 1896, nearly five months after the women's demonstration in Zaragoza. It provided specific information about the activities of a woman acting as a Sister of Charity in Cuba, Doña María Luisa Raya y Villaroel, who spent eight months on the island. The young woman went to Cuba to avoid being separated from her husband, Don José Pando Alcazár, assigned to head the Wad-Ras battalion. When she left Madrid on the train for Cádiz, she spotted a small group of country women, mothers of soldiers who were going off to war. Doña María addressed the women from the window of her first-class carriage: "'Don't weep,' she said to them; 'I am going with the men and I shall care for them'" (No lloren Uds, —les decía;— yo también voy con ellos y los cuidaré). In Cuba she served, as Blanco tells her story, as a Sister of Charity for her husband's battalion, which she accompanied at all times, even into combat. She cooked and tended to the wounded under the most trying circumstances. Eventually, she became ill and had to return to Spain. At the end of his article Blanco avoided the sentimentality that normally suffused descriptions of the services rendered by the Sisters of Charity in Cuba in order to refer explicitly and bitterly to the dire consequences Doña María and, by implication, other sisters faced:

> After those days spent in the midst of the rudest combat, bullets no longer endanger her life. But this fragile creature could not evade the illnesses common in a land where the strongest organisms are destroyed.
>
> The pretty young woman seen in the Mediodía railway station, the happy Madrilenian who cheered up the mothers of departing soldiers, the Sister of Charity in the field of battle, is returning to the peninsula just as those soldiers return who receive commissions [monetary assistance] from *El Imparcial*, that is to say, ill, ravaged by anemia, nearly dead.
>
> Después de aquellas jornadas, en medio de los combates más rudos, las balas no han vuelto a hacer peligrar su vida. Pero no podía salvarse este

ser débil de las enfermedades de una tierra donde los organismos más fuertes se destruyen.

La linda señorita de la estación del Mediodía, la alegre madrileña que animaba a las madres de los soldados, la Hermana de la Caridad en el campo de batalla, regresa a la Península como regresan esos soldados que reciben las comisiones de *El Imparcial,* enferma, destruida por la anemia, casi sin vida.

Blanco's interpretation of Doña María's actions in Cuba emphasized her courage under fire and her willingness to expose herself to disease, in addition to her womanly compassion. Moreover, the fact that this privileged woman returned to Spain in the same wretched condition as the poor soldiers who received small amounts of much-needed money raised by *El Imparcial* from reader subscriptions pointedly drew attention to the irrelevance, under certain circumstances, of class and gender in a war that demanded extreme sacrifice primarily from poor men.

The prevailing persistent and comforting vision of women as angels of mercy during the first insurrection as during the second uprising was counterbalanced by the disturbing images of poor mothers who watched their sons depart, perhaps forever. In 1869 Gervasio Amat's play *Quintas y caixas* mirrored popular protest against the inequity of conscription by describing the hardships imposed on poor farmers when young male laborers were sent off to the war.[18] *¡Viva Cuba española!* an 1871 zarzuela by Isidoro Martínez Sanz—reprinted in 1896 by the author's son of the same name and retitled *Familia y patria*—in effect exhorted Spaniards to fight wherever they were sent despite the tears shed by loving mothers. The play aimed to reconcile family interests with the demands of the fatherland and urged that mothers, regardless of economic circumstances, could best contribute to this goal by letting sons go to war without protest. Women's relationship to war in these plays was couched either in economic terms—the repercussions of losing a family member who was a source of support—or in terms of self-sacrifice enjoined upon them by sentimental or patriotic propaganda.

\*   \*   \*

### WAR IN MELILLA

In an essay published in 1982, "Women as Mirror and Other: Toward a Theory of Women, War, and Feminism," Jean Bethke Elshtain theorized that women in the context of modern war may be considered as Mirror and as Other, a categorization that is suggestive of but only partially applicable to nineteenth-century Spain. Spanish history and tradition do include women, such as Agustina Aragón, who in specific circumstances temporarily mirror male warriors' single-minded determination to defeat the enemy: they are admired and deemed worthy of emulation. A woman like Catalina de Erauso also mirrors male warriors, but her motivation and conduct (and that of those who imitate her closely) cannot be examined too carefully since such an examination might reveal monstrous anomalies of the kind Palacio Valdés embodied in his María: she represents a type that clearly threatens to transgress gender boundaries. Nonetheless, as noted above, in the context of the 1895–98 wars against Cuba and the Philippines Catalina was invoked in the press as a model whose significance no one seemed eager to probe very deeply.

With the possible exception of the protestors against conscription during the colonial insurrections, it is difficult to find women, whether real or imagined, who embody Elshtain's Other, that is, projections of aspects of an increasingly complex male psyche that men want to suppress—charity, humility, tenderness, pacifism—since they may lead to doubts about the legitimacy and conduct of war. The plight of noncombatant women victimized by unjust wars, such as Arenal's women and Cabrera's mother, could, of course, lead some men to reflect on such wars, on their true causes and consequences and on their folly.

In 1893 war broke out against Muslim tribes inhabiting the area near the Spanish enclave of Melilla in North Africa. The conflict began when the Spanish government ordered the construction of a fortress on disputed land outside Melilla. The fort was to be built next to a mosque and a cemetery that held the remains of a revered Muslim cleric. Neighboring Berber tribes were ignored when they demanded that the fort be moved to another location. They proceeded to attack the workers and soldiers at the construction site. A brief war ensued, from September 29, 1893 to March 5, 1894, during which Spanish conscripts were called up in the usual way, that is, by lottery. Those who could afford to buy their way out of military service did so. The poor had no choice but to serve or desert.

Three months after the war began, Rosario de Acuña, a playwright who had gained notoriety as a freethinker with her 1891 play *El Padre Juan*, premiered her fifth play, *La voz de la patria*, at the Teatro Español in Madrid. Rosario de Acuña had won the rare distinction of being the first woman playwright to have a theater closed down, following the premiere of *El Padre Juan*. In 1885 she had publicly joined the ranks of freethinkers when she began writing for *Las dominicales del Libre Pensamiento* (Acuña 1989, 7, 12, 14). This anti-Catholic and anticlerical republican paper was considered to be the voice of Masonry. It was directed by the Aragonese journalist Ramón Chíes, and one of its correspondents was Odón de Buen, the University of Barcelona professor of natural sciences whose Darwinism drew fierce attacks from the Catholic Church in the autumn of 1895.[19] On February 20, 1886, Rosario de Acuña was inducted into a Masonic lodge in Alicante, an event covered by the local press. Odón de Buen wrote of her: "Doña Rosario de Acuña was an extraordinary woman [. . .]. Endowed with a very lively personality, very firm in her ideas, she suffered the most impassioned persecutions, and she was not left in peace even toward the end of her life, which she spent in the north of Spain in retirement, although she never stopped advocating the ideas she professed among the people around her there" (Doña Rosario de Acuña era una mujer extraordinaria [...]. Muy viva de carácter, muy firme en sus ideas, sufrió las más apasionadas persecuciones y no se le dejó en paz ni en las postrimerías de su vida, que pasó retirada en el norte de España, aunque no olvidando la propaganda entre los que la rodeaban, de las ideas que profesaba) (2003, 68).

The importance of Masonry in the thought and actions of Rosario de Acuña and like-minded women of this period cannot be overemphasized. Libertad Morte notes that there was a resurgence of Masonic activity beginning in 1874 owing to the liberalizing influence of the First

Republic. By 1894–95 there were seven *logias de adopción* (lodges for women) under the authority of the Gran Oriente Español. Women also figured in the lists of some male lodges and attended meetings alongside men. The work undertaken in the women's lodges was the same as that undertaken by men in theirs. The eminent historian of Masonry in Spain Ferrer Benimeli cites a significant toast offered on April 5, 1889, in a Madrid lodge by Ángeles López de Ayala to her fellow Mason Alfredo Vega, Viscount of Ros, Grand Master of the Grande Oriente Nacional, "who dignified women by elevating them to the same level as men, and by recognizing their rights, which is a favor and not an act of justice given the ignorance of most women at the present time." And she added: "A great step has been taken toward the emancipation of women in general [. . .]; Masonry will be the redeemer of our sex" ("que dignificaba a la mujer elevándola al igual del hombre y reconociéndola los derechos de la personalidad, lo cual es favor y no justicia, por la ignorancia de la mujer en general." Y añadió: "Se ha dado un gran paso hacia la emancipación de la mujer [...]; la Masonería sera el redentor de nuestro sexo").[20]

Rosario de Acuña's history suggests that the title of her 1893 play, *La voz de la patria*, is ironic. Moreover, for a modern reader its opening scenes seem to furnish a fictional example of Elshtain's proposed figure of the woman as Other. The Aragonese mother in the play makes a case against letting her son go to war by challenging the use of abstract terms such as *honor, fatherland,* and *glory.* She argues that the survival and happiness of the flesh-and-blood family is what matters to her and that it is what ought to matter to men as well. Twenty-two years earlier, Eloy Perillán de Buxo and Pedro Marquina had built their drama *El sitio de París* (1871) around the question of how the siege affected a particular French family. His protagonist, Marieta, voices ideas similar to those of the mother in Rosario de Acuña's play. Told that her husband died having fulfilled his duty, she cries: "You presume to say this to a woman wounded to the quick? To a widow bereft of consolation? He fulfilled his duty! You are among those who, trampling the natural laws of sentiment and profaning the laws of love, believe that the fatherland is worth more than the affection of a wife, more than the peace found within the family, more than the kiss bestowed by a son! How are men to be good patriots when they do not begin by being fathers!" (¿Y sois vos quien tal dice a la mujer herida en el corazón? ¿a la viuda sin consuelo? ¡Cumplía su deber! ¡También sois vos de los que, atropellando las leyes naturales del sentimiento y profanando las del amor, creéis que la patria vale más que el cariño de una esposa, más que la paz de la familia, más que el beso de un hijo! ¿Cómo han de ser buenos patriotas los que empiezan por no ser padres?) (67). But later on, Marieta herself plunges into battle: "Very well: I too shall go with you. You have told me that beyond the Pyrenees there is a noble nation called Spain where more than once, virile women, covering the corpses of their husbands with their own bodies, forced the eagles of Empire to retreat! . . . I wish to imitate them. My friends! Let us avenge our husbands, let us go to our deaths!" (Pues bien: yo también iré con vos. ¡Me habéis contado que detrás de los Pirineos hay una hidalga nación que se llama España, donde más de una vez, las mujeres varoniles, cubriendo con sus cuerpos los cadáveres de sus esposos, hicieron retroceder las águilas del Imperio!... Yo quiero imitarlas. ¡Compañeras! Vamos a vengar a nuestros maridos, vamos a morir!) (74–75). The speeches of the women in these two plays illustrate a pattern familiar in the representation of Western women's response to war. First there is heartfelt rejection of war for the sake of the family, followed closely by acceptance of war and even participation in war for the sake of national honor and personal revenge.

The husband in Rosario de Acuña's play counters his wife's position with a charge often heard in stories and plays written in the 1890s in which mothers try to dissuade their sons from going to war. The charge is that mothers are by nature too attached emotionally to their sons to think clearly about military service. A mother's love for a son is flawed by her inability to reason and her lack of judgment. And that makes a mother's love potentially pernicious: unchecked, it may lead sons to forsake the pursuit of honor and the good of society. At worst it can lead to a life of enslavement to the limited and timorous aspirations of an unalloyed female vision of life.

These often-repeated charges leveled by men at mothers are expressed by a neighbor woman, Rosa, as well as by the husband. Rosa is a woman who has fully accepted the validity of men's attitudes toward war, along with all the words they use to justify it. When she is asked what the word *fatherland* means to her, she proudly demonstrates that it is not an empty word: it is where she was born, where she lives, where she converses with others in a language they all share. While the mother is opposed to all wars and does not appear to care that the war in Melilla is being conducted against Muslims, Rosa finds it intolerable—as does the husband—that offenses against Spanish honor have been committed by Moorish "dogs." Just as a woman, Rosa, shares the husband's views on war, so does a man, Antonio, share the mother's. He considers war barbaric, in brutal opposition to what ought to be the true goal of life, the pursuit of concrete well-being.

In the end, the mother's attempts to persuade her son to desert fail. He announces to the assembled characters that he has overcome the momentary weakness caused by his mother's "womanish over-protectiveness" (mujeril desvelo) and will go to Africa. When Rosa offers him her scapular, his father urges him to take it, to indulge the "infantile innocence" (candor infantil) of women to whom is owed affectionate indulgence. The mother and Antonio are ultimately overwhelmed by the patriotic fervor displayed by the entire town in which they live. The mother capitulates to the husband and bestows a formal blessing on her son.

What is significant about *La voz de la patria* is that while the author classified it as a "patriotic" play, it is also a work in which ideas and attitudes about war seldom, if ever, expressed at the time by women (or men, for that matter) in Spanish fiction were aired in public, least of all in the commercial theater and press. The questioning of terms such as *honor, fatherland,* and, by implication, *patriotism* was bold. Similar questioning was, of course, taking place among workers and political dissidents both in Spain and abroad. For example, on November 15, 1893, a workers' paper, *El Despertar* (The Awakening), published in New York from 1891 to 1902, further developed these ideas: "The *fatherland,* the disastrous idea of the fatherland is surfacing again and it threatens to bring lamentations and desolation to the dwellings of workers. It is useless for mothers to weep: *offended national honor* cries out for the extermination of the enemy and men throw themselves into the fray lusting for flesh . . . which the bourgeoisie will eat up later, converted into hard, cold cash" (La *patria*, la funesta idea de patria, surge de nuevo y amenaza llevar el llanto y desolación en hogares obreros. Inútil que lloren las madres: el *honor nacional ofendido* reclama el exterminio y allá se lanza el hombre sediento de carne... que se comerán después los burgueses, convertido en oro contante y sonante) (Núñez Florencio 1990, 142).

How, one wonders, did contemporary viewers interpret the mother's silence concerning the religion of Spain's antagonists in Melilla set beside Rosa's vocal contempt for the Moorish "dogs"? The perception, fostered and echoed in most of the conservative and liberal press alike, was that Spanish honor had been offended by the disobedience and rebellion of an unworthy (i.e., Muslim) people. Press coverage of the war makes clear that Rosa was, in fact, echoing ideas and sentiments in circulation at the time. There was much discussion of outraged honor, with frequent references to the *rifeños*, in racist language.[21] That the Catholic mother—unlike Rosa—does not seize upon the difference in religion as a factor in justification of the war marks a departure from the conventional way in which Spanish Catholic women were represented in regard to military confrontations with the infidel.

In effect, the mother in Rosario de Acuña's play never raises the question of whether the conflict in Africa constitutes a just war. She remains silent on this question, in contrast to the vocal position taken by the press and perhaps by many contemporaries who were encouraged to view it as a war justified for religious reasons, if not a just war in Arenal's terms.[22]

It is noteworthy that as recently as 1859–60, during a brief war in Morocco, Queen Isabel II had herself aspired to rise to the level of a unifying force in a deeply divided country by emulating the first Isabel as a defender of the faith. Her piety and spirit of self-sacrifice— she offered to sell all her jewels to further the goals of such a "holy undertaking"—apparently won her the admiration of the people (Carr 1982, 261; Medio 1966, 194). Nonetheless, the stirring example of nation and queen united in a common effort against the Muslim enemy faded away after Isabel was forced to abandon the throne and go off into exile in 1868. Spaniards did not invoke the memory of her role in the Moroccan war in the 1890s, when women's participation in war and the conduct of national affairs became a subject of discussion.

The action in Melilla had significant consequences. Fernando Puell de la Villa (1996) argues that soldiers who no longer listened to republicans, whose promises to abolish the abuses of the *quinta* had come to nothing, did listen to anarchists and socialists. These groups took advantage of the deficiencies of the Melilla campaign to urge soldiers to question the utility and necessity of military service, as well as the very existence of the army. Puell de la Villa also notes that General Weyler concluded that the deficiencies of the operation heartened the Cuban insurrectionists who acted two years later (257–58).

# CHAPTER TWO

# Women and Violent
# Political Actions

> If its enemies had numbered as many women among its ranks as men, the government at Versailles would have had a harder time of it; it is only just to recognize that our male friends are more susceptible to pleas for compassion. Woman, who is supposedly faint of heart, is better able than men to say, It must be! It tears her apart, but she remains impassive. Without hatred, without anger, without pity for herself or others, it <u>must be,</u> whether or not her heart is bleeding.
>
> That is what the women of the Commune were like.
>
> LOUISE MICHEL, *Mémoires*

## THE PARIS COMMUNE

By the summer of 1896 and then throughout and following the resolution of the two colonial insurrections, women's relationship to war had become an increasingly inevitable component of the wider discourse on the "Woman Question" and feminism in Spain and elsewhere. The role played by women in violent uprisings such as the Paris Commune or in anarchist terrorist actions became part of this discourse and raised similar questions. Only twenty-six years had elapsed since the Paris Commune, which contemporaries perceived as drastically colored by women's participation. Contemporary journalists, essayists, and illustrators emphasized the role of female incendiaries in the events that erupted in Paris from March 18 to May 28, 1871. The historian Daniel Pick (1989) connects their perceived role to subsequent theorizing on the nature of the crowd voiced by Gustave Le Bon and Gabriel Tarde:

"Women were seen by Le Bon and Tarde, the other best-known French crowd theorist of the late-nineteenth century, as not only the passive victims, but also the active agents of revolutionary disorder. From the image of the *tricoteuses* of the 1790s, to the *petroleuses* of 1871, women were cast as the quintessential embodiment of political anarchy" (92–93). Gabriel Tarde, whose theories often appeared with commentary in the Spanish press—always attentive to new currents in French thought—went so far as to identify the crowd as female in his book *Opinion et la foule* (1891): "By its routine caprice [. . .] its credulity, its excitability, its rapid leaps from fury to tenderness, from exasperation to bursts of laughter, the crowd is woman, even when it is composed, as almost always happens, of masculine elements" (Pick 1989, 195).

The connection drawn between women and disorder, destructiveness and chaos, in the aftermath of the Franco-Prussian War and the Commune reached a memorable apogee in a play by Alexandre Dumas fils, *La femme de Claude*, first performed in 1873. The play was revived in Paris in 1894 and reviewed on September 21 of that year by L. Arzubialde in *El Imparcial*. The reviewer explained that the characters in the play were symbolic: Claude represented work, honor, Man, the Citizen, while the woman he killed (played by Sarah Bernhardt) was not the adulteress who embittered his existence and mocked his love but rather the unworthy creature, the indocile, frivolous, venal siren. The embodiment of female perversity, she was the devourer of lives and honor, the spirit of Evil, the lascivious Beast of the Apocalypse whom Dumas had beheld at the outset of the 1870 war, weakening, grinding down, destroying France and retarding the march of Humanity toward the grandeur of the Ideal. Arzubialde characterized the play's "philosophy" as "mystical-patriotic." While it is not clear what he meant by this term, his explication of the symbolism behind Claude's wife provides a vivid (and unquestioned) image of woman as a formidable agent of destruction.

What were the communards thought to have done? José Álvarez Junco (1971) has gathered together a useful collection of contemporary Spanish news reports and illustrations that offer accounts of the women's actions and reflect perceptions of them. One such article from a Spanish liberal-conservative paper reported that women and boys taken prisoner confessed that they had received money for throwing tins containing a flammable mixture of petrol, grease, and sulfur (67). The article continues:

> By now it is notorious, and a thousand facts that one report cannot set forth prove that women and children were the most ardent perpetrators of the work of blood and destruction carried out in Paris.
>
> On many barricades fifteen-year-old girls were found standing erect upon the paving stones reddened by fire, exciting men to combat.
>
> Many officers have been killed by women, by female officers of women workers' collectives, by store clerks, by seamstresses.
>
> Several female workers employed in a shoe factory in the Faubourg Montmartre [. . .] poisoned soldiers yesterday, inviting them to take a drink of something cool. A multitude of country women have been shot for starting fires.

> Es hoy notorio, y mil hechos, que una correspondencia no basta a agrupar, prueban que las mujeres y los chicos han sido los más ardientes agentes de la obra de sangre y destrucción que en París se ha llevado a cabo.
>
> En muchas barricadas se hallaban muchachas de 15 años que excitaban al combate, erguidas sobre los adoquines enrojecidos por el incendio.
>
> Muchos oficiales han sido muertos por mujeres, por oficialas de obrador, por dependientes de almacén, por modistas.
>
> Varias obreras empleadas en una zapatería del faubourg Montmartre [...] han envenenado ayer a los soldados, invitándoles refrescar. Multitud de mujeres del pueblo han sido fusiladas como incendiarias. (67)[1]

Lurid accounts of the women's actions, supplemented by images of communards that emphasized their combativeness, appalled Spanish conservatives, while emboldening communists, socialists, and anarchists, who welcomed women as participants in revolutionary struggle. Many anarchist and socialist newspapers reviewed the events and significance of the Commune every year. Moreover, meetings held annually in Spain on March 18 by anarchists and socialists to commemorate the Commune emphasized the presence of women at these events.

For example, *El Socialista* noted on March 28, 1897, that various cities and towns in Spain had reported to the newspaper on the nature of the ceremonies and the sex of participants at those meetings.

Recent scholarship on the Paris Commune—Gay Gullickson's *Unruly Women of Paris* (1996), Robert Tombs's *The Paris Commune, 1871* (1999), and Carolyn J. Eichner's *Surmounting the Barricades: Women in the Paris Commune* (2004)—has modified earlier versions of women's role. Gullickson identifies the significance of women's participation in the Paris Commune thus:

> It was also . . . a defining moment for Western conceptualizations of gender, not least because it gave birth to the powerful, evil, and imaginary *pétroleuses* (female incendiaries) who were accused of setting fire to Paris during the semaine sanglante. Exercising a powerful grip on the Western cultural imagination, the *pétroleuse* became the negative embodiment of the publicly active woman and cast a long shadow over debates about women's rights and proper roles. Although no longer well-known by name, versions of the *pétroleuse* continue to shape our understanding of the past and remain a touchstone for Western notions of gender. (3)

Time-honored representations of the communards have long defied modification. Robert Tombs dedicated a section of his study to the question, noting that "few if any now believe that *petroleuses* set fire to houses or gave poisoned drinks to soldiers"; nonetheless, he writes, some historians persist in portraying the women as dedicated to the violent overthrow of "bourgeois morality" by forming armed battalions and manning barricades. He concludes, as do Gullickson and Eichner, that there is no evidence for these assertions. (Eichner does believe that some women may have manned barricades, but her principal concern is with women's political organizing, not their active participation in fighting.) In effect, Tombs argues that the historical record shows that women performed as they have traditionally performed under wartime conditions—as canteen bearers, nurses, support for the men. Yet, if the violence once attributed to the communards no longer holds up to scrutiny, their insistence on playing a role in public affairs has never been disputed. This aspect of their conduct was well understood by Spanish conservatives at the time.

In a women's publication backed by the prolific writer Faustina Sáez de Melgar the charge leveled against the communards shortly after the uprising in 1871 was that they were "mujeres desalmadas" (women without souls). Meanwhile, women were urged in the same Catholic, monarchist publication to learn something about political life, not with a view toward direct participation in it, but rather so as to "redeem" fathers, husbands, friends, and sons from extreme partisan positions.[2] The influence of the Catholic Church and the monarchy guaranteed purity of motives in women, who were thus encouraged to act as untainted guides to beneficent political action to be effected by men.

In the Spain of the 1890s conservatives' recollections of female violence in the Commune, mistaken though they were, remained sufficiently vivid to make men wary of women who wanted to participate in public life. This stance chimed in with the position sanctioned by the Catholic Church and the monarchy and accepted by right-thinking women as well as men.

## WOMEN ANARCHISTS

Historians of anarchism in late-nineteenth-century Spain have documented the relatively slight attraction it had for women. Temma Kaplan (1987) underscores the hold the family and the Catholic Church had on Spanish female anarchists by providing them with some power and even a measure of prestige: "But male anarchists persisted in their attacks on both church and family without offering alternatives. Anarchists did not provide or promise desperately needed social services that women might control themselves. Unless male anarchists could create new opportunities for communalism to replace the old social structure and until they could create enclaves of power for women within the movement, there was no way to win masses of women supporters" (402). The historian of Spanish feminism Geraldine Scanlon shares this view of the hold religion had on many anarchist women in the 1890s and later (1976, 256).[3]

Yet, despite the apparent inability of anarchists to recruit and retain large numbers of women, the sudden appearance of female anarchists on the national scene in the early summer of 1896 appeared to pose a serious threat. Women composed a significant number of those imprisoned in connection with a bomb attack directed at a Corpus Christi procession on a street in Barcelona, Cambios Nuevos. The June 7 attack caused six to twelve deaths (accounts differ) and left forty-five wounded. More than four hundred people were arrested and confined in the dungeons of the Montjuich fortress, used as a military prison.[4]

A report in *El Imparcial* on June 27, 1896, recorded the scandalized reaction of the Sisters of Charity, who supervised the women, to their prisoners' behavior, which they said was "so inappropriate for their sex." Some of the women blasphemed, while the thirty-four-year-old anarchist Teresa Claramunt tried to drown out with her shouts the prayers of those who were devout. When she was forcibly restrained, she reportedly complained loudly at being compelled to witness religious observances: "I am an anarchist," she exclaimed, "and I shall always be an anarchist. I shall never stop believing what I believe now. You can burn me, if you like, but my ashes will create and strengthen elements favorable to the triumph of my cause" (Soy, exclama, anarquista y lo seré siempre. No dejaré nunca de pensar como pienso. Pueden, si quieren, quemarme; pero mis cenizas crearán y fortificarán elementos favorables al triunfo de mi causa). Three years earlier, Claramunt's fellow anarchist Emma Goldman, detained in a Philadelphia jail on suspicion of inciting to riot, had been handed a Bible by the matron. "It recalled to my mind the cruel face of my religious instructor in school. Indignantly I flung the volume at the matron's feet. I had no need of religious lies; I wanted some human book, I told her. For a moment she stood horror-stricken; then she began raging at me. I had desecrated God's word; I would be put in the dungeon: later on I would burn in hell" (Goldman 1931, 125). Glimpses such as these into the ill-contained rage some anarchist women felt at the imposition of religious practices and material on unbelievers are valuable since many other anarchist women, especially in Spain, found it difficult to break away from religious practices and conventions.

Five of the twenty-six individuals who were convicted in the Cambios Nuevos bombing were executed. Twenty-two were given maximum penalties but were later freed, in 1900, in response to international pressure, while the rest were banished from the country (Pierats 1990, 10). Claramunt was the only woman said to have suffered torture during her confinement in Montjuich (her account of her jail experience is in the appendix). She went into exile, first to France and then to England.[5]

Several anarchist women, Claramunt among them, used the stage as well as the anarchist press to propagandize for their cause. On April 25, 1896, one of the best known of the communards, Louise Michel, wrote to Felipe Cortiella, director of the Compañía Libre de Declamación, in Barcelona, giving him permission to produce *La huelga* (The Strike). Because of the repressive climate following anarchist attacks in that city, the play was not performed (Litvak 1981, 236). A few weeks earlier, on March 14, 1896, Claramunt's play *El mundo que muere y el mundo que nace* (The World That Is Dying and the World Being Born) had been performed in Barcelona by Cortiella's company, but it had been denounced almost immediately to the appropriate magistrate and closed down, at least temporarily (Litvak 1981, 240–41).[6]

It is worthy of note that when Emma Goldman published *The Social Significance of Modern Drama* in 1914 she did not mention Michel, Claramunt, or Rosario de Acuña, despite her broad and frequent contacts with European anarchists and their propagandizing efforts. Goldman wrote that until Githa Sowerby made her appearance with *Rutherford and Son* (1912) "no country had produced a single woman dramatist of note" (Goldman 1987, 130). Goldman believed that drama could be a weapon for raising political awareness, although she was critical of plays that sacrificed art to ideology. While it is not possible to measure the influence of the plays by Michel, Rosario de Acuña, and Teresa Claramunt referred to here, it is probably fair to say that they raised public awareness of their messages simply by drawing the attention of the censors.

The anarchist press supported the women's demonstrations in Zaragoza, as did the socialists. Carlos Serrano, in *El final del imperio* (1984, 244), reprints an article from the anarchist *El Corsario* of July 23, 1896, in which the Zaragoza women are encouraged to persist in their complaints. The paper reported that on July 17 the women had applied for permission to stage a demonstration, but their request had been turned down. The article in *El Corsario* continues: "Hurrah, mothers of Zaragoza! Modern Spartans! We congratulate you for this initiative worthy of being supported by all of Spain. Today your sons are sent off to a cemetery called Cuba: let us stop them by all means possible. 'Cuba for Cubans, Spain for Spaniards' [. . .]. Do you see, now that you are trying to protest these shipments worthy of slave traders in which the sons of workers are piled up like cargo, that any sign of protest is forbidden to you?" (¡Hurra, madres zaragozanas!; nuevas espartanas modernas; os felicitamos por esa iniciativa digna de secundar por toda España. Hoy vuestros hijos son lanzados a un cementerio llamado Cuba: detengámonos por todos los medios. "Cuba para los cubanos. España para los españoles"[...]. ¿Véis ahora que tratáis de protestar de esos embarques propios de negreros, en los que sirven de hacinada carga los hijos de trabajadores, como se os prohíbe toda señal de protesta?) The article concludes with an appeal for support in behalf of the women of Zaragoza: "Let the protest be unanimous, and we shall prevail" (Sea unánime la protesta y venceremos).[7]

Encouragement from the left had little impact, while the mainstream Spanish press in general disapproved of women taking political action, especially when it was motivated by considerations of class. "Instantáneas: Feminismo," an article on the impact of feminism, appeared in *El Globo* on August 25, 1896, less than a month after the women's demonstration in Zaragoza and barely two months after the Cambios Nuevos bombing. Its author, Ovejero, referred specifically to the long list of women imprisoned in Barcelona for suspected complicity in the anarchist cause, but he warned more generally of the dark consequences for Spanish society of female political action. He portrayed women who engaged in political action as deviating from their proper gender roles and, in some instances, breaking away from the restraints of religion.

Spanish anarchists were obliged to consider new strategies for the future by the autumn of 1896. As had already happened in France, laws were enacted to suppress anarchist actions and propaganda. In the French Republic laws passed after the assassination of President Carnot on June 26, 1894, made advocacy of anarchism an offense. There were to be no trials by jury for anarchists and no outlets for propaganda, including press reports (Weber 1986, 116–17). On September 2, 1896, the Spanish parliament approved a law of repression aimed at anarchists and terrorists that provided for military jurisdiction over infractors. The law allowed the suppression of social centers and workers' newspapers, as well as measures that could be taken against foreign agitators who entered Spain. By the early twentieth century the violent period of individual acts of terrorism and anarchist actions initiated in the late 1880s had come to an end (Termes 1986, 18).

# CHAPTER THREE

# The 1896 Women's Demonstrations against Conscription

Regarding all the statements made this afternoon against the vote for women, I am bound to say, with all due respect, that they are not supported by reality. Let us take some of them at random. For example, when did women rise up to protest the Moroccan War? First, why didn't men protest? Second: who, except for women, protested and rose up in Zaragoza at the time of the Cuban war? [. . .] Women! How can you say that when women give some signs of life indicating that they will work on behalf of the Republic they will be given the vote as a reward? Haven't women already fought for the Republic?

CLARA CAMPOAMOR, "Discurso ante las Cortes el 1 de octubre de 1931"

## THE WOMEN'S DEMONSTRATION IN ZARAGOZA

War, as Jean Bethke Elshtain has argued in *Women and War* (1987), cannot be conducted without the cooperation of women. Spanish women were clearly expected to cooperate in the war effort by expressing solidarity with government policy through public demonstrations of support. Anything less could provoke criticism. On April 26, 1896, Rafael Gasset wrote an editorial for *El Imparcial* assuring readers that Spanish newspapers were read in Cuba. Including reports on the tears shed in public by Spanish mothers distraught at sending their sons off to war, on the financial problems occasioned by the war, and on the exhaustion and lukewarm public spirit evinced toward the war would surely provide comfort to the enemy, who might then resist peace overtures. "That is why it would be doing Spain grave damage to go about sniveling for peace" (He aquí por donde se puede hacer un grave daño a España lloriqueando la paz).

Women were often depicted as guardians of a moral virility—masculine power engaged with issues of morality—in the service of the unquestioning acceptance of war and its consequences that some men had forfeited. For example, on May 15, 1896, an editorial in *El Imparcial* praised the gallant cheerfulness Spanish women displayed while doing their duty compared with the unmanly and unpatriotic conduct of Italian males: "While in Milan men were going to the station to prevent the departure of a train carrying troops to Eritrea, here women went to cheer up the expeditionary battalion with their smiles and hurrahs" (Mientras en Milán los hombres iban a la estación del ferrocarril a impedir que saliera un tren que llevaba tropas a Eritrea, aquí iban las mujeres a animar con sus sonrisas y con sus vítores al batallón expedicionario).[1] Comments of this kind clearly fostered the existence and increase of the "militarized masculinity," which Joshua S. Goldstein, among others, argues is essential for the gendered conduct of war (2001, 251–331). Women throughout the nineteenth century periodically shamed men into assuming their consecrated role.

Moral admonitions and flattery directed at women, mothers in particular, were not entirely effective, as events soon demonstrated. Two weeks before a delegation of three women in Zaragoza formally requested permission to demonstrate, General Arsenio Martínez Campos, who had recently been relieved of his command in Cuba, spoke before the Spanish Senate. He concluded his remarks by sending a heartfelt greeting to the soldiers fighting on the island and to the mothers of those valiant soldiers, whose patriotism, he averred, knew no limits. His audience responded with bravos (*El Imparcial,* July 2, 1896). Nevertheless, in Zaragoza on July 17 the limits of some mothers' patriotism became evident when they presented the interim governor, Sr. Ballester, with their written request for permission to demonstrate. The governor, Martínez del Campo, who had been in Madrid, returned immediately to take charge of an investigation into their request. According to a press report in *El Imparcial* on July 18, 1896, the request stated that a group of women wanted to protest the projected transport of additional forces to Cuba, which would include more of their sons, thus leaving them destitute. The interim governor denied the request. The minister of the interior and the minister of war immediately telegraphed Zaragoza for further information about the proposed demonstration. Official quarters ascribed it to revolutionary agitation *(trabajos revolu- cionarios)* carried out by the enemies of Spain and expressed confidence that patriotism would prevail. The correspondent for *El Imparcial* in Zaragoza reported that the whole city knew about the women's request; some Zaragozans remarked that there were families in the area all of whose sons were in the army. It should be noted that since the women who presented the petition to demonstrate could not read or write, they had enlisted the help of a *memorialista,* who redacted the document. That individual was summoned to Martínez del Campo's office for questioning, but he was released for lack of evidence connecting him to any conspiracy.

The women's request prompted an editorial in *El Imparcial* the following day, July 18. The piece is significant first of all because, considered together with the ministers' immediate demand for information, it clearly indicates that the proposed demonstration was taken seriously and was in no way regarded as a minor incident in a provincial city. In fact, the editorialist viewed the request as nothing less than the first sign of a change in the national conscience. And, he wrote, the prime minister himself, Antonio Cánovas, had stated on more than one occasion that the national conscience would point the way to the resolution of the conflict in Cuba. That such a request should be made in Zaragoza, one of the proudest and most patriotic of all Spanish cities, was astonishing. As for the women, the editorial speculated that the blind love of mothers for their offspring had given rise to this first sign of alteration in the national conscience and that it was likely that the women did not understand how their request had led to this change.

During the days before the women demonstrated without permission, on August 1, *El Imparcial* reported that the authorities had sought, located, and interviewed the individual who drafted the request but had not discovered those who were assumed to have conceived the plan to demonstrate. The women themselves claimed that they had acted on their own, without outside influence or control. Although a dispatch filed from Zaragoza by El Imparcial's correspondent on July 21 referred to a local paper's claim that everyone there knew that a *filibustero* club was active in the city, officials in Madrid and Zaragoza stated that the incident now appeared to be without importance.

On July 25 El Imparcial, which had until then used the heading "Protest in Zaragoza" for its brief communiqués from that city, entitled four related news items "The Question of Public Order." The first item revealed that leaflets entitled "Down with the war," urging soldiers to refuse to go to Cuba, had appeared on July 23 enfolded in the anarchist paper *El Corsario*. Antiwar material addressed to tavernkeepers for distribution to their working-class customers had been sent through the mail. Several deserters, captured while on their way to the French border, appeared in Zaragoza on their way to jail in that city, raising the possibility of moral contamination occasioned by their very presence.

The second brief notice informed readers that signs of trouble had appeared elsewhere and thus the authorities had begun to crack down on the press. In Valencia, Belén Sárraga, a committed freethinker, anarchist, Mason, and feminist propagandist, was arrested. Sárraga, born in 1874, was a teacher and journalist who had founded the Federación de Grupos Femeninos de Valencia in 1895. In 1897 she cofounded the Asociación General Femenina, located in Valencia. In accord with an anarchist drive to educate workers, she also organized a society of women, mostly field laborers in the countryside around Málaga, which numbered about twenty thousand members (Brenan 1962, 165). According to Lola Iturbe (1974, 64), during the second Cuban insurrection Sárraga traveled throughout Valencia enlisting women to demonstrate against the war, promoting Cuban independence and the restoration of the republic. It was in her capacity as director and founder of the anarchist paper *La Conciencia Libre* that she was detained and her documents were confiscated.[2] Finally, the report in El Imparcial added that in Barcelona a newspaper thought to be sympathetic to *filibusteros* had been seized and that in Alicante the authorities had detained individuals who were distributing material deemed subversive of the war effort.

At 12:10 p.m. on August 1, El Imparcial's correspondent in Zaragoza filed a detailed description of what had happened earlier that morning (the report appeared in *El Imparcial* on August 2). A small group of women, he wrote, had formed in the Plaza of San Felipe and headed for the Plaza Grande del Mercado. Passing along San Pablo Street, they had been joined by curious onlookers. At the Plaza of San Pedro they had tied to a cane a cloth with the colors of the Spanish flag that bore the inscription "Long live Spain! Let no more troops go to Cuba! Let the poor and the rich go!" Many more women had joined the demonstrators there, and they had all continued on toward the *alpargata* (canvas sandals) factory. The women factory workers had come out and joined the protest. At that point, and no earlier, wrote the correspondent, a police chief had told the group to disperse, but they had continued on along Castellana Street, where the women workers from another shop had joined them. When they had approached the civil government building, the inspector of public order took away their flag. Throughout the march, wrote the reporter, the women had cried "Long live Spain!" along with other "meaningful" shouts.

The large crowd that had formed by this time gathered before the civil government building and protested when the police detained a woman "who stood out for her animated conduct," together with a man who was cheering the women on. The protestors had marched to the police station to demand the release of the two individuals, at which point the police tried again to disperse them. Some of the women had left the crowd in order to head for the hat factory on the outskirts of the city, where they meant to ask for support from the women workers there. But the chief of police, Sr. Imputar, had managed to reach the women before they arrived at their destination. He had arrested two men, two women, and two young fellows who were among the noisiest of the demonstrators. In view of the police chief's action, the other women had dispersed, vowing to return in the afternoon.

The *Imparcial* correspondent ended his report by asserting, first, that the townspeople had been indifferent to the demonstration, which was, in any case, headed primarily by women whose interest in demonstrating was unclear since they were mere girls and old women, and, second, that the march had been part of a coordinated effort by agitators. This was evident, he wrote, because some of the demonstrators had said that there were going to be protests in Barcelona, Valencia, and Madrid that very day.

At 10:10 that same night (August 1) the correspondent wrote again, noting that the women detained and questioned by the police did not have family members in Cuba, an observation that again raised questions about the reasons for their participation. He also repeated his claim that unseen others had been behind the "antipatriotic campaign," which, he also repeated, had in fact attracted a piddling number of protestors against the "tribute of blood."

*El Imparcial* supplemented the two reports with an update on the government's position on events in Zaragoza. The ministers of war and the interior announced that the number of demonstrators was not believed to have exceeded fifty in all, most of them boys and young girls. Behind these individuals had been *filibusteros*, who with the aid of one or another extremist newspaper aimed to cause disturbances in port cities from which soldiers embarked for Cuba. Public opinion was grounded, fortunately, in the purest patriotic sentiment and was unlikely to echo the propaganda voiced by the Zaragoza demonstrators.

On the following day, August 2, the correspondent for *El Imparcial* provided the names of six of the forty or so protestors who had been detained by the police: Eusebia Cristóbal, twenty-four; Isabel Piña, fifteen; Isabel Fulle, who had carried the flag during the demonstration; Antonio Domínguez; Angel Saldaña; Tomás Casanau; and the child Esteban Pano. All but Antonio Domínguez and Angel Saldaña claimed that they had joined the protest when they saw it pass by but had not been part of it. Domínguez and Saldaña were sent to jail. The correspondent noted that the local press had condemned the march and trusted that the authorities would put an end to such demonstrations. He noted further that men had not sympathized with the women protestors. One of them, he reported, had remarked as he saw some of the women march by, "What are their husbands thinking? It's a shame they don't give them a good beating!" (¿Qué hacen los maridos? Lástima que no las arrimaran un buen estacazo) (*El Imparcial*, August 3, 1896).

This casual reference to violence as a means of control over women, apparently sanctioned by the speaker as a husband's duty in some instances, is the only reference to domestic violence I have turned up in contemporary discussions or representations of connections between women and various forms of violence. Like the comparison of the Zaragoza protestors to foolish female goats noted below, this reference betrays the unthinking acceptance and no doubt deliberate perpetuation of stereotypes of women that supposedly justified their correction by men. In her 2006 collection of essays, *Are Women Human? And Other International Dialogues*, Catharine A. MacKinnon argues that the international system is hypocritical in recognizing some crimes against humanity while failing to confront similar crimes when they happen to women, often on a daily basis. Torture, for example, is commonly believed to involve the use of violence to control and intimidate, but when violence is used to control and intimidate women in domestic situations it is not called torture or conceptualized in the same way. MacKinnon writes that we recognize war as a process in which people are killed and maimed fighting over land and power, but when women are raped and beaten up by men, we somehow manage to place the phenomenon in a different category. "It is hard," she continues, "to avoid the impression that what is called war is what men make against each other, and what they do to women is called everyday life" (274).

If it is difficult for many people in the twenty-first century to draw the connection MacKinnon makes, it was doubtless inconceivable for Spaniards to do so at the end of the nineteenth century. Domestic abuse, counted a misdemeanor, was not uncommon in Spain. The Penal Code provided that a husband who beat his wife without causing lesions could be sentenced to fifteen days in jail, fined from five to fifty pesetas, and given a reprimand. But according to Emilio Langle Rubio (1911, 115–16), punishment was rarely imposed upon batterers since the abused woman herself had to file charges and women, accustomed to their subservient status, were reluctant to do so.

On August 3 *El Imparcial* printed the suggestion that an unnamed Protestant minister, a native of New York with Cuban connections, had been behind the demonstration. Three days later the popular *El Imparcial* columnist Mariano de Cavia concurred with an article published in *El Correo* that warned against charging Protestants with a conspiracy for which there was no evidence. On the other hand, Mariano de Cavia wrote, Jews, who were bleeding Spain dry, did pose an "imminent danger." Typical of the widespread anti-Semitism of the time, Cavia's remarks about covetous Samuel Levis were as unsubstantiated as those about Protestants, to which he objected. Cavia was not alone among reporters and columnists in warning against Jewish interests. José Ortega Munilla devoted most of a column in *Los Lunes de El Imparcial* on August 10, 1896, to Spain's unfortunate need for the help of the "sinister figure of Samuel" to finance the Cuban war. He quoted the text of a cartoon depicting a Christian and a Jew running after a piece of money, a race the single-minded Jew always wins. That, Ortega wrote, is what makes "Samuel" feared and odious. On August 26, 1896, in his paper, *El Pueblo,* published in Valencia, Blasco Ibáñez voiced fears about Jewish control of Spanish resources and the exploitation of Spanish labor. Blasco frequently denounced "Jewish rapacity."[3]

*El Imparcial* on August 3 also printed a dispatch from Valencia reporting that Belén Sárraga de Ferrero, director of *La Conciencia Libre,* had been tried and sent to jail for publishing two articles, "What are the people waiting for?" (¿Qué espera el pueblo?) and "Let the example spread" (Que cunda el ejemplo). Four days later, on August 7, the "Bourgeois Week" (Semana burguesa) section of *El Socialista* noted that the second article was a reprint of one it had published weeks earlier without incident. *El Socialista* observed further that the columnist for *El Imparcial* who alluded to a Protestant pastor as the figure behind the demonstration had insulted the women of Zaragoza by calling them *caloyas,* a word used in Aragón to refer to the goat's humble and foolish female mate.

### THE SIGNIFICANCE OF THE WOMEN'S DEMONSTRATION

How did contemporaries gauge the significance of the demonstration in Zaragoza? For José Ortega Munilla, editor of *Los Lunes de El Imparcial* (the weekly literary supplement to the daily *Imparcial*) and father of the journalist and intellectual José Ortega y Gasset, the words *women* and *Zaragoza* placed in juxtaposition conjured up the exalted model of patriotism familiar to all Spaniards. Demonstrations funded by foreign money and dependent on the participation of girls too young to have sons could not undermine that model. The well-known abuses associated with conscription could not account for the march, since those or similar abuses also had existed during the War of Independence and had not discouraged abnegation on the part of the mothers of Zaragoza or prevented them from engaging in heroic acts. Ortega Munilla put his faith in the virtue of the race. When faced with great challenges, Spanish women would rise to the level of patriotism displayed by their forebears (*Los Lunes de El Imparcial*, August 3, 1896).

Not all commentators shared an interpretation of the events in Zaragoza that questioned the sincerity of the women's opposition to conscription and even to the war. Emilio Castelar, a former president of the First Republic and an indefatigable contributor to *El Globo* and *El Liberal* during the nineties, confided his misgivings concerning the demonstrations in a letter to a friend on August 4, 1896. He believed that the protest begun in Zaragoza against the conscription's unequal treatment of rich and poor was spreading. Indeed, on August 7, 1896, *El Socialista* reported that there had been an attempt to hold a demonstration in Chiva, an important town in Valencia. Castelar reminded his friend that the First Republic had put an end to the evasion of service through payment, only to have it put back in place under the Restoration. He concluded that it was very likely—if God did not resolve the issue—that just as the Carlist war against the republic had brought in the monarchy, this republican war against the monarchy would bring in the republic (Castelar 1908, 344). The elderly statesman who had devoted his life to the instauration of the republic now considered it the worst of all possible evils (Núñez Florencio 1990, 275).

Fear of the collapse of public order and subsequent revolution prompted an editorial in *El Imparcial* on August 6, 1896. Antigovernment bands in Valencia—"sparks" of revolutionary activity—had just made their appearance and, together with the march in Zaragoza, made it imperative that the government quench the spreading fire at once. The editorialist warned against assuming that *filibusteros* were behind the demonstrations, in the same way that some had assumed that the hidden hand of Catholic reaction had been behind the Carlist Wars. It was necessary, he believed, to probe more deeply into several possible causes. Above all, it was important to act quickly since other nations were observing Spain, watching for signs of internal dissension. In the concluding paragraph the editorialist clearly revealed his fear that, faced with continuing disturbances, the government would act in its own interest and not in the interest of the Spanish people. The writer implied that the interest of the government essentially amounted to its survival at any cost.

By August 5 pro-Cuba papers in Paris were reporting on the women's demonstrations: *El Imparcial* of August 5 noted that *L'Intransigeant* and other papers in the French capital had published pieces favorable to the women and their cause. The *New York Times* and the *New York Herald* took note of the riots in Valencia and women's participation in them in early August, repeating the government's claim that the riots had been instigated by Cuban insurrectionists. The *New York Times* did not fully accept the official explanation that the riots had been started by troublemaking *filibusteros,* considering them the result of excessive taxation and unjust conscription policies: "The riots in Spain are a symptom of very serious popular discontent with the course of the government in respect to Cuba" (*New York Times,* August 7, 1896). International coverage of these events was a source of concern for the Spanish government, which feared that any sign of weakness concerning its control over the population exposed the nation to harm.

On August 7, 1896, *El Imparcial* reported that the women testifying in the hearings in Zaragoza had all claimed that they had acted on their own initiative. The correspondent remarked that they had probably been coached to say this but said that public opinion continued to ascribe the demonstration to concealed "germs of *filibusterismo.*" In a further attempt to control the press, the judge in the case ordered the trial of the former director of the weekly *El Bombo,* Antonio Domínguez (not, presumably, the Antonio Domínguez who had been sent to jail on August 2). On August 10 it was discovered that he had fled Zaragoza (*El Imparcial,* August 11, 1896).

Blasco Ibáñez, a staunch republican, supported the demands of the women of Zaragoza in *El Pueblo*. An article titled "Carne de pobres" (The Flesh of Poor People) appeared on August 19, 1896, launching a campaign against the *quinta* that echoed the cry of the Zaragoza protestors. "¡Que vayan todos: pobres y ricos!" (Let all go, the poor and the rich!). A similar demonstration had been attempted a few days after the Zaragoza march in Chiva. In reference to the Chiva protest *El Socialista* commented on August 7, 1896, that it showed that the Zaragoza demonstration was spreading its message urging an end to the war or at least the establishment of a more just conscription policy. On August 22 *El Imparcial* reported that some women in Viso de Alcor (near Sevilla) had carried out a demonstration the previous day analogous to the one in Zaragoza. The women had marched to the town hall and demanded that no more sons be sent to war and that the war be ended in some other way. The correspondent averred that the inhabitants of the town deplored the demonstration. When still another demonstration took place in Valencia on August 22, Blasco compared it to the earlier march in Zaragoza and again defended the women against the charge that *filibusteros* were behind their protest. Titled "Los verdaderos filbusteros," his article appeared in *El Pueblo* on August 24. Despite his efforts, Blasco's articles reportedly had little impact (Serrano 1982, 203–4). One year later, on August 6, 1897, Blasco published an article in *El Pueblo* in which he wondered at the silence of the two hundred thousand mothers of soldiers sent to Cuba and the Philippines. The dissent sparked by women in the summer and fall of 1896 appeared to him to have dissipated. Meanwhile, many conscripts manifested their opposition to the war by silently deserting. Their number rose from 4,853 men in 1895 to 9,676 in 1897 (Núñez Florencio 1990, 295).

When Prime Minister Antonio Cánovas addressed Parliament on August 21, 1896, he identified one cause alone for the recently discovered conspiracy in the Philippines: the demonstration in Zaragoza and the disturbances in Valencia. He did not allude to a demonstration that had taken place that same day in Viso del Alcor, in which women had demanded that the war be ended in some other way than by sending more sons to fight. (The Viso del Alcor march and Cánovas's speech before Parliament were both reported in *El Imparcial* on August 22, 1896.) Cánovas told the parliament that Cuban *filibusteros* had provoked all of these events in order to distract Spain from its goal, which was to defeat the Cuban insurrection. He then referred to attempts made in Barcelona to maintain the pitch of agitation by having people shout "Let the poor and the rich go to Cuba!" and vowed to take whatever steps were necessary to maintain public order.

The patriotic line on how to view the inequities of the recruitment policy and consequently on how to assess the significance of the women's protest was expressed in an editorial by José Ortega Munilla in *El Imparcial* on August 31, 1896, less than a month after the Zaragoza demonstration. Ortega marveled at the fact that despite the errors of ministers and generals, and despite the efforts of *filibusteros,* recruits were still filling the trains to the Transatlántica steamships, on which they embarked for Cuba and the Philippines. That miracle of patriotism, he wrote, was being enacted by the very men who benefited least from Spain's social and economic organization, by men who only registered the existence of the state when the tax collector appeared or a sergeant arrived to fill the *quinta:*

> Perhaps history registers nothing like it. The scoffing at eternal principles that has demoralized the middle class and the upper class has not been able to destroy the people's heart of gold, which wholly belongs to Spain.
>
> Once again the brave soldier lad sets out, a bit confused with the emotion of the leave-taking, certain that when he sacrifices his life he will be complying with the most glorious of duties.
>
> He expects no compensations; he neither desires nor needs them. He does what he does because his conscience orders him to in a confused and poorly understood voice, but one so energetic that it leaves no room for doubt. He is going to fight as his father fought, as his grandfather fought, in this eternal Spanish war to which we seem condemned without remission.

> Acaso no registre la historia ejemplo semejante. La burla de los eternos principios que ha desmoralizado a la clase media y a las clases superiores, no ha podido destruir el corazón de oro de la plebe, que es todo entero para España.

Ahora va otra vez el soldadito, un poco aturdido con las emociones de la despedida, lleno de entusiasmo, seguro de que al sacrificar su vida cumple el más glorioso de los deberes.

No espera recompensas, ni las desea, ni las necesita. Lo que hace lo hace porque se lo manda su conciencia con voz confusa y mal entendida, pero tan enérgicamente, que no le deja lugar a duda. Va a pelear como peleó su padre, como peleó su abuelo en esta perdurable guerra española a que parecemos condenados sin remisión possible.

The socialists, who had been consistently vocal in opposition to a recruitment system that permitted the well-off to evade service with a cash payment, ran an editorial in *El Socialista* on September 4, 1896, a few days after Ortega Munilla's, that included the statement, "While the sons of the people go off to shed their blood for the Mama Land, the offspring of the aristocracy employ their leisure by holding amateur bullfights in which they take part as matadors" (Mientras los hijos del pueblo van a dar su sangre por mama patria, los chicos de la aristocracia distraen sus ocios celebrando becerradas en las que toman parte como lidiadores). On September 19 the socialist newspaper in Bilbao, *La Lucha de Clases,* called upon Spanish mothers to persevere in opposing the war, and on September 25 an editorial in *El Socialista* stated the following:

> The only ones who up to now have suffered the hazards of war are the poor. More than two hundred thousand have gone to Cuba. Who knows how many more are yet to go and how many will be needed to confront other conflicts?
>
> We send the soldiers off with music, speeches, *vivas*, bishop's blessings and . . . tears; when they return wounded, sick, or disabled, they're welcomed back by lowbred swindlers if they have any money, or if they don't they're forced to beg . . .
>
> The people are asked for more and more men. No protests are tolerated, not even the request that there be no special privileges. It has come to the point that men who evade service by emigrating are defamed, while others continue to evade it with money.

Los únicos que hasta ahora han sufrido los azares de la guerra son los pobres. A Cuba han ido más de 200,000, ¿quién sabe los que habrán de ir aun y los que serán necesarios para afrontar los demás conflictos?

Se despide a los soldados con músicas, discursos, vivas, bendiciones episcopales y... lágrimas; se los recibe cuando regresan heridos o inútiles, por timadores de baja estofa, si traen dinero, o han de pedir limosna si de él carecen...

Al pueblo se le piden hombres y más hombres, sin tolerar protestar ni aun pedir que no haya privilegios. Se llega hasta infamar los que eluden el servicio de las armas con la emigración como otros lo eluden con el dinero.

The socialists continued their campaign on the national level against the inequities of the *quinta* from mid-1897 on, increasing the number of their meetings and broadening distribution of their propaganda.

For its part, *El Imparcial,* with its much higher circulation (still only about one hundred thousand buyers out of Spain's population of seventeen million), provided accounts of the suffering endured by poor mothers because of unjust recruitment practices. For example, on May 22, 1898, the paper reported the precarious situation of Petra Múñiz de la Osa, a widow with three sons. One had served in Cuba, where he was wounded three times and was finally discharged for disability. The second was serving in Cuba. The third had been called up even though he was the only son left to support his impoverished mother. The report commented that to deprive Petra of the son who was attending to her needs was to condemn her to death by starvation. It ended by asking, "Will the Minister of War give his consent to such an iniquitous action?" (¿Consentirá el señor ministro de la Guerra tamaña iniquidad?).

Although some press reports and observers had minimized the significance of the women's demonstrations in August 1896, choosing to portray the women as the dupes of Cuban, Protestant, or other interested agitators, there were, as noted above, other thoughtful observers who perceived the women demonstrators as conscious harbingers of a growing, generalized discontent with the government and its conduct of the war against the Cuban insurgents. Anarchists, communists, republicans, and patriots of all political stripes reacted as if they accepted the idea that the women were consciously seizing the occasion, taking advantage of a combination of volatile political circumstances to make their dissent visible. In the event, none of their supporters managed to construct a collective protest movement to back up the women's efforts. Nor were coordinated conspiracies successful. Stanley G. Payne (1967) notes a republican attempt to foment revolt that sought to ride the wave of discontent publicized by the women of Zaragoza. He refers to the women's demonstrations during the summer of 1896 and writes that "Republican conspirators hatched a plot with sergeants in several peninsular garrisons to provoke an anti-government mutiny, but this was discovered, and more than twenty sergeants were expelled from the Army" (76).

One of the soldiers quartered in Barcelona, Manuel Ciges Aparicio, later recalled his state of mind and that of his fellow soldiers during that August of 1896 as they awaited orders to leave for Cuba. He considered it cowardly of the nation not to have backed the Zaragoza women's demonstration since in his view Spaniards did, in fact, support them. Rather than viewing it as antipatriotic, he and his comrades had thought it appropriate to protest that "abominable war," which only devoured the poor. In his account of those days preceding the soldiers' departure, Ciges Aparicio described the agitated scene he witnessed in the city: Sheets were circulated urging soldiers not to embark. Men approached the soldiers as they walked about in their striped uniforms, saying, "Don't board the ship. Let the rich go. . . . Let the ones who started the war go." Women urged them to desert: "Don't board the ship, my son." Girls came up to them with the same message. Ciges Aparicio contacted his family to send money so that he could escape to France, but it didn't arrive in time.

The soldiers in Ciges's company had plotted to stage a revolt on the wharf at the last moment, but their arms were taken from them to be kept in the ship's hold in order to guard against rusting, and the plan was foiled. On August 24, 1896, Ciges was one of 410 men who were marched through the heavily policed streets of Barcelona to the wharf, where armed guards monitored them as they prepared to board the transatlantic *Buenos Aires* for the voyage to Cuba. Silent protestors were only able to show opposition by the expressions of sadness on their faces. A voice cried out "Long live anarchy!" and the soldiers embarked (1986, 257, 271, 413).

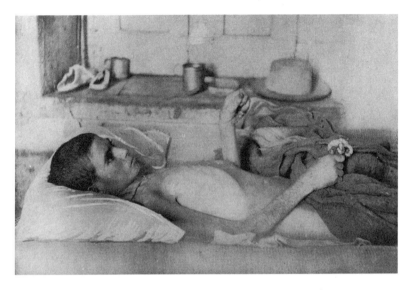

*Greater America*. New York: F. Tennyson Neely, 1898. A dying reconcentrado boy in the hospital of the American Orphans in Havana.

*La Ilustración artística* (1896): 255. Photo of Elsa Tobin,
married to the Spanish general Arola. Tobin, born in Leeds,
wore this military uniform (often called "amazon garb") as
she met each boatload of Spanish troops in Havana and
distributed money and flowers to them.

*La Ilustración artística*, no. 727 (December 1898): 807. Barcelona: Embarkation of the Barbastro battalions and the light infantry of Mérida, expeditionary forces, to Cuba on November 23, 1895. A view of the Barceloneta wharf, site of the embarkation. (From the photograph by Xatart.)

*La Ilustración artística* (1897): 487. Barcelona: Disembarkation of
wounded and sick soldiers arriving from the Philippines.

*Ilustración española y americana* (1898): 45. "Joy and bitterness."

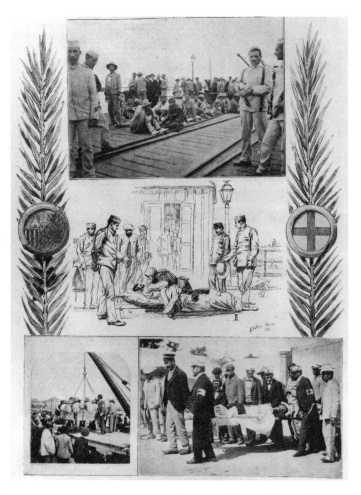

*La Ilustración española y americana,* September 8, 1898,
no. xxiii, pp.129, 130, "Repatriation."

*La Ilustración artística* (1896): 704. Photo of the staff of the Havana daily,
*El Comercio. Front row, left to right:* Eva Canel, Ernesto Lecuona, and López
Seña. *Back row, left to right:* Daniel Martínez, Martín Lamy, Carlos Carrió,
Pedro Giralt, Ramón Garí, Federico Rosainz.

*Greater America.* New York: F. Tennyson Neely, 1898. Santo Suarez is the principal relief station in Havana. For a while, until the outbreak of war with the United States, four thousand reconcentrados were daily supplied with food, medicine, etc., here.

# CHAPTER FOUR

# Institutions That Shaped Women's Lives

Carlota: Men want us removed from political life so that we cannot reform their iniquitous laws. For them freedom and the world; for us resignation and obedience. But I do not complain as much about men as I do about women themselves. My mother is a woman, and she is a despot in her treatment of me as my father, were he still alive, might not be.

Julia: Nature made us free; religion and laws made us slaves. I laugh at all those who say that Christianity emancipated us women.

*El Nuevo Régimen*, September 29, 1900

## WOMEN AND SUFFRAGE

In the midst of widespread discontent women protestors, simply by virtue of their sex, succeeded in dramatizing the inequity of the conscription system. They captured the attention of the entire country and beyond. Their actions were undoubtedly registered by some of their compatriots as meaningful symptoms of resistance, but their legal status, which included formal exclusion from the political process as voters and officeholders, marked them essentially as chattels of their male relatives and husbands, thus minimizing the impact of their participation in political actions. As things stood, the electoral process was not an avenue to participation in politics for either men or women at the end of the nineteenth century. There were very few male voters during this period. Moreover, during the first fifteen years of the Restoration the restrictive suffrage laws imposed by Cánovas prevented the working classes from voting. In 1886 only 2.1 percent of the total population voted (Martínez

Cuadrado 1969, 222). In 1899, nine years after the passage of universal male suffrage in 1890, the Spanish sociologist Adolfo Posada wrote:

> The suffrage in Spain can scarcely be called such; it exists in law, but in practice it is an indecorous and unworthy farce. Vitiated from the outset, corrupted in practice, a clumsy mockery in its implementation, suffrage for us is a shadow of what it should be; for all of us who ascribe ethical value to patriotism, the suffrage in Spain is a source of national shame. Since this is so, how is it possible for men to feel the necessity of giving it to women, or for women to want to obtain a right that is illusory at times, uncomfortable at other times, and almost always ineffectual and impotent? Women surely cannot be in a hurry to become . . . mere honorary voters like the great majority of Spanish men, nor does it occur to anyone that women will be in a position to exercise political influence in the state by obtaining the vote.

> El sufragio en España apenas puede llamarse tal: existe en la ley, siendo en la práctica una farsa indecorosa e indigna. Viciado el voto en su origen, corrompido en su ejercicio, torpemente burlado en sus manifestaciones, es el sufragio en nosotros sombra de lo que debía ser; para cuantos damos al patriotismo un valor ético, un motivo de vergüenza nacional. Ahora bien: siendo el sufragio así, ¿cómo sentir la necesidad de concedérselo a la mujer? ¿Para qué quiere ésta un derecho cuyo ejercicio es ilusorio unas veces, otras incómodo y casi siempre ineficaz e impotente? Ni la mujer puede sentir prisas por ser elector... honorario, como lo son la inmensa mayoría de los españoles electores, ni a nadie se le ocurre que con el sufragio adquiera hoy la mujer una condición favorable, para sentir el influjo de su criterio político en el estado. (222–23)

Despite reflections such as these, the vote for women was, of course, on the long-range agenda of most feminists in Spain, male and female alike. Catholics who may have been inclined toward women's suffrage in the next few years were, however, constrained by the opposition of Pope Pius X (1903–14) to women's being voters and officeholders: "women ought to limit themselves solely to awakening the consciousness of civic duties in their sons" (las mujeres sólo deben limitarse a despertar en sus hijos la conciencia de los deberes cívicos) (Fagoaga de Bartolomé 1985, 112).

## WOMEN'S EDUCATION, THE LAW, AND THE CATHOLIC CHURCH

Equally important as the vote and more fundamental for the immediate future was education. Although compulsory primary education had been instituted in Spain in 1857, on October 13, 1897, an editorial in *El Imparcial* asserted: "Our system of education is deficient, according to the latest census. Out of eighteen million inhabitants, eight and one half million can neither read nor write—almost half the population— and this is the case despite the existence of sixty thousand teachers and twenty-five thousand primary schools") (Nuestra enseñanza pública es deficiente, según el último censo. De 18 millones de habitantes, ocho y media no saben leer ni escribir; es decir, casi la mitad, y eso que tenemos 60.000 maestros y 25.000 escuelas públicas). Lack of state funds left two-thirds of secondary education in the hands of the teaching orders (see the final selection in the appendix, by Teresa Claramunt). Thus, education at the secondary level was an option reserved largely for the elite. As for women, their rate of illiteracy in 1900 was 71.4 percent, compared with 55.8 percent for men. Few women were able to obtain more than a primary education, and those who did attended normal schools or general and technical institutes (Palacio Lis 1992, 31). From 1880 to 1890 only twenty women studied in Spanish universities (Fagoaga de Bartolomé 1985, 64). Concepción Aleixandre, the first practicing Spanish woman doctor, told Clara Campoamor—elected a deputy to Parliament in 1931, she worked for women's rights to divorce and the vote on equal terms with men—that in 1896 male students routinely threw rocks at her when she emerged from the School of Medicine (Campoamor 1939, 13). It should be noted that in the neighboring French Republic there were 7 female doctors as of 1882, 95 by 1903, and only 556 by 1928 (Weber 1986, 95; Perrot 1987, 52–53). Changes in social consciousness, in the legal system, and in education were imperative if there were to be changes in the perception of women in public life.

In 1919 Margarita Nelken, a socialist, later a deputy to Parliament, called for changes in the Spanish Civil Code, which considered women as eternal minors or incompetents: "Syndicates, associations formed to protect working women, will all be useless so long as a woman cannot defend her interests, not only with the permission of her lord and master but also, when necessary, against that very lord and master, and whatever feminism does will fail unless the Civil Code remedies the shameful situation in which a woman is placed when she marries" (Sindicatos, asociaciones para protección del trabajo femenino, todo será inútil mientras la mujer no pueda defender sus intereses, no sólo sin la venia de su dueño, pero también, en caso necesario, contra este mismo dueño y cuanto haga el femenismo fracasará mientras una reforma del Código Civil no suprima la vergonzosa situación en que el matrimonio coloca a la mujer) (Nelken 1975, 175).

The Spanish Civil Code of 1889 decreed that men should protect women and that women should obey their husbands. A woman had to reside where her husband wished. The husband administered the couple's assets and represented his wife. A woman had to obtain her husband's permission to engage in any civil action and was not allowed to own a business (Nash 1983, 160). She had to obtain her husband's permission in order to publish her work (Urruela 2001, 162). Again, for the sake of comparison, it should be noted that in France, until it was modified in 1907, the Napoleonic Code allowed a husband to receive the royalties on a wife's work, own the copyrights, and dispose of them as he saw fit (Thurman 1999, 517n22).

In 1911 Emilio Langle Rubio published *La mujer en el derecho penal*, a study of the Penal Code of 1870, which was still in effect, as it related to women. His examination of the document clearly demonstrated that women were constrained to obedience by the 1889 Civil Code and punished by the Penal Code for any hints of rebellion against the lord and master whom marriage imposed on them. He concluded that the law must change so that women would no longer be the slaves of men, but rather their companions (118, 120).

In the meantime, reformers working to improve secular education for women were reminded of the precariousness of their undertaking by an article written for *El Globo* on March 31, 1896—four months before the Zaragoza demonstration—by the president of the Asociación para la Enseñanza de la Mujer, Manuel Ruiz de Quevedo, in which he detailed how the bishop of Madrid, Sr. Alcalá, was attempting to scuttle funding for the institution. The Asociación, founded by Fernando de Castro in 1870, was intended to provide an education for women similar to that offered six years later by the Institución Libre de Enseñanza. The Asociación welcomed the cooperation of all Spaniards regardless of their religious, philosophical, or political ideas. Members of the governing junta, as well as instructors, represented a wide range of beliefs. Dependent on outside sources of funding, the Asociación had received financial and other help from the government in the past and had recently been promised a subvention of five thousand pesetas. According to Ruiz de Quevedo, before the former minister of development (fomento), Alberto Bosch—who had stepped down in December 1895—had signed the subvention document, the bishop of Madrid had visited the prime minister, Antonio Cánovas, in order to lodge an objection to the granting of the funds. Cánovas had forwarded the bishop's complaint to Bosch. In a conversation with Ruiz de Quevedo, Bosch had reasoned that the government's wish to accommodate the bishop in this matter was related to the cooperation lent by the Catholic Church to the government's war against the Cuban insurrectionists. Bosch had specifically cited the papal nuncio's address on the occasion of the military review of troops in Vitoria.

About one month later, on May 2, 1896, Ruiz de Quevedo furnished a report to *El Nuevo Régimen* claiming that the government intended to deprive the Asociación of official support so that it would founder. Reactionary elements, according to the author, were successfully pressing the case against granting the five thousand pesetas to the Asociación and were also mounting a propaganda campaign to undermine public support for the institution. In the event, the Asociación did not disappear: in September 1896 it numbered 194 pupils, not counting the primary school, with room for 120 (*El Globo*, September 30, 1896). The successful struggle to survive despite the hostility of the Catholic Church in cahoots with the government was crucial, as the Asociación para la Enseñanza de la Mujer offered girls and young women the best education available in Spain in the nineteenth century.[1]

The extreme antagonism of radical elements within the Catholic Church toward civil liberties—for men as well as women—is illustrated by the notorious work published in 1885 by Felix Sardá I Salvani, *El liberalismo es un pecado (Liberalism is a Sin)*. The teachings in this book were supported and further promulgated in the catechism of P. Mazo, which went through twenty-nine editions by 1900, and by the Jesuit Gabino Márquez in the twentieth century. Sardá I Salvani denounced almost all civil liberties, including secular education. In his book he posed the questions, "what other freedoms does liberalism advocate? [the response] freedom of conscience, freedom of religion and the press . . . [and] are there other pernicious freedoms? yes, sir, academic freedom, freedom of information and of assembly . . . [and] why are these freedoms pernicious? because they serve to teach error, propagate vice, and work against the Church" (¿qué otras libertades defiende el liberalismo?: la libertad de conciencia, la libertad de cultos y de imprenta... [y] ¿hay otras libertades perniciosas?: sí, señor, la libertad de cátedra, de propaganda y de reunion... [y] ¿por qué son perniciosas estas libertades?: porque sirven para enseñar el error, propagar el vicio y maquinar contra la iglesia) (Miret Magdalena and Sádaba 1998, 11).

### WOMEN'S GRADUAL ENTRY INTO POLITICAL LIFE

Avenues to political involvement for women gradually opened up. As had always been the case, some women braved the hostility of their own and the opposite sex in order to attend rallies and meetings. And they demonstrated. For example, on April 3, 1898, twelve days before the United States declared war on Spain, socialists and republicans led by some of the most prominent members of these parties marched in Madrid. By the time the demonstrators reached what is now the Prado Museum, they numbered more than three thousand people. The reporter who covered the event noted that he had seen some twenty women participants. The marchers presented the civil governor with a list of demands that included reexamination of the Montjuich trial, of obligatory military service, and of the regulations governing the importing of wheat (*El Imparcial*, April 4, 1898). In 1909 women were active participants in the Tragic Week uprising in Barcelona, which was triggered in part by antiwar sentiment and protests against conscription. Women fought in the streets alongside men and instigated convent burnings.[2]

Increasingly, women made their voices heard as writers of fiction and as journalists addressing themselves less exclusively to a female audience. As they gained visibility outside the home, especially as journalists, the perception of their public role slowly began to change. Women like Emilia Pardo Bazán and Eva Canel, who wrote for papers in Latin America and Cuba as well as in Spain and did not hesitate to air their opinions on war, divorce, education, and other matters vital to the discussions being held in the public sphere, were significant voices for change. Shortly after the turn of the century, Carmen de Burgos earned a reputation as Spain's first female journalist.[3] She was a prolific writer of polemical fiction and nonfiction, writing in favor, most notably, of divorce. In 1909 the *Heraldo de Madrid* assigned her to Melilla as a war correspondent. Although like Eva Canel before her, she did not actually observe and write about combat, she did comment on the conditions endured by the soldiers, the state of hospitals, even the lives and opinions of the enemy. At the very least, a woman was present at a war, voicing her reactions to what she saw in a major Madrid newspaper.

# CHAPTER FIVE

# Women's Voices

> "What are people saying?"
> "And the soldiers? What do they say?"
> "And young people?"
> "And old people?"
> "And mothers?"
> "Mothers have no more tears. They have shed so many that their souls are dry, and all they feel is rage. The tide is rising; patience is exhausted; something huge is crystallizing in the public consciousness. What is going to happen? Will the government act in unison with this sentiment?"
>
> *La Ilustración Española y Americana*, 1898

## WOMEN'S DEMONSTRATIONS

In the twentieth and twenty-first centuries women have continued to march as did the women of Zaragoza. Results are mixed and often long in coming, but the women who marched regularly in the Plaza de Mayo in Buenos Aires to protest government torture and the "disappearance" of suspected political dissidents in the 1970s and 1980s and the Ladies in White *(Damas de Blanco)*, who marched in Havana's Revolutionary Square to protest the lack of medical care for incarcerated dissidents in the summer of 2004, testify to the fact that women marching in public places continue to embarrass and inconvenience those in power.[1] Autocratic, patriarchal governments are typically at a loss as to how to handle the women they place on pedestals away from the conduct of political action when the women step down and begin marching.

Most important, they cannot prevent other nations from witnessing the unwelcome spectacle.

In early 2005 an independent Cuban reporter wrote that the demonstrations conducted by the Ladies in White constituted the most significant event of 2004 in Cuba. He cited José Martí's gallantry—"No cause is impossible when a woman puts her heart and soul into bringing it to fruition" (No hay causa imposible cuando en ella se alista el alma de la mujer)—and concluded his article thus: "At times, in order for an act of autocratic folly to be overturned it is necessary that a new social movement be preceded by white vestments clothing the body of a woman" (A veces para que una locura autocrática se derrumbe hace falta que ese movimiento social venga precedido de un vestido blanco, cubriendo el cuerpo de una mujer).[2] While it is true that the Cuban women gave interviews and expressed their aims in writing as well, a woman's body remained the crucial image for the Cuban journalist.

An emphasis on women's bodies in protests such as these may garner attention and concentrate the minds of observers on a particular cause, but it may also have the effect of enhancing men's sense of difference, of affirming a sense of privileged masculinity that allows them to justify their domination of women. Such a sense of difference, amounting to a conviction of natural superiority, depends in part on the contrast between female bodies, which are perceived to be bound to biological functions (menstruation, childbearing), and men's bodies, whose superiority is thought to derive largely from their freedom from such functions. In fact, on August 1, 1896, the *Imparcial* correspondent covering the protest in Zaragoza questioned the motivation of the women, noting that they were "mere girls and old women," that is, too young or too old to have sons subject to conscription. Since they were not motivated by the biological ties of motherhood, their protest could not be valid. From this perspective, women who act and think based on the imperatives of their biological functions—the wives and mothers of the Plaza de Mayo demonstrations and the 2004 Ladies in White—can be taken seriously as women acting in accord with their assigned roles, while women who are perceived as acting outside the guidelines handed down for their sex may be seen as imposters. It was thus plausible for some contemporaries to define the women protestors in Zaragoza in general as the objects of manipulation by subversive elements hostile to Spain.

## MISSING VOICES OF WOMEN

Missing from the above account of women demonstrators in Spain are the voices of the women who demonstrated. Their impact as well was apparently and necessarily focused on the display of their female bodies. What were the women thinking? What were their thoughts about the government whose conscription policy they opposed? Widespread female illiteracy (71.4 percent were illiterate in 1900) prevented many women from expressing themselves in print; it is known that the women who requested permission to demonstrate in Zaragoza could not write.[3] We are obliged to look for clues to their thoughts and attitudes in the images drawn by men in popular journals and to the fiction, plays, and zarzuelas, also, for the most part, written by men, which often reflected the thoughts and emotions of the popular classes.

A class focus appeared in two stories published, respectively, in *Los Lunes de El Imparcial* on February 24, 1896—Leopoldo Alas's bitter sketch "El rana"—and in *El Socialista* on October 15, 1897—Emilia Pardo Bazan's story "Poema humilde." Alas's story deals with the heartless treatment accorded those volunteers from the lower classes who had signed up for duty in Cuba out of abject poverty. The story is particularly worthy of note for its explicit criticism of the Catholic Church's indifference to the departing volunteers. The church is represented as viewing them as nothing more than scraps of humanity to be swept away by the Cuban war in what amounted to a welcome housecleaning. Pardo Bazan's story describes the plight of a humble rural couple separated by the war. The young man, whose father failed to have him exempted from service with a bribe, must leave for Cuba. He returns wounded and dies on the dock as soon as he lands.

Of the fair number of stories and poems written about conscription and its consequences during this period, one of the most compelling is Alas's "El sustituto," which appeared in *Los Lunes de El Imparcial* in 1893.

The story is set in 1893, during the brief war in Melilla. A poor widow with four children owes a large amount of back rent to a well-off land-owner whose son draws a low number in the conscription lottery. The landowner, who is short on cash, pulls all the strings at his disposal in order to get his son exempted from service, but he does not succeed in his attempts. As it happens, a solution does lie at hand: he will forgive the back rent owed him by the widow provided her oldest son goes to Africa as a substitute for his only son. She refuses, saying that she would rather end up on the street with all four of her children than send her son to war. But her son himself accepts the offer and dies soon after of fever contracted in Africa. The landowner's son experiences such intense guilt over his death that he goes to Africa himself, assuming the substitute's identity. He dies a heroic death, which, happily, guarantees a pension to the widowed mother. While this tale focuses in transpar-ently didactic fashion on the guilt of the man who accepted a substitute and only indirectly on the mother, it did provide a strong argument against a draft policy that forced people to make drastic, tragic choices.

Images of wives, mothers, and daughters bidding farewell to depart-ing soldiers or greeting their maimed husbands, sons, and fathers on their return are common in the illustrated journals of the time.[4] They are meant to elicit sympathy and do not represent the women as con-frontational in any way. That is not the case in some of the zarzuelas performed during and immediately after the second Cuban insurrec-tion. One of the playwrights who focused on the plight of poor women and their sons did give the women a voice, however belatedly. Pascual Millán wrote ¡Quince bajas! (Fifteen Casualties!) in 1896, but it was not performed until December 3, 1898, and it was closed the following night by order of the civil governor, allegedly because military officers in attendance objected to its depiction of the Spanish soldier. In fact, the play's real offense lay in its portrayal of the Spanish government as callous and unjust in the implementation of its conscription policy. Millán presented a rural mother, Petra, complaining to the mayor of her town about the government and lamenting her son's imminent departure for Cuba. The mayor responds that the fatherland always comes before one's son. To which she replies, "The fatherland! What does the fatherland matter to me? What's certain is that if Gaspar does not come back, it won't be the fatherland that weeps for him, and the fatherland won't be coming here to sow seed in the land in his place!" (¡La patria! ¿A mí qué me importa eso? ¡A fe que si no vuelve Gaspar, no será la patria la que le llore ni la que le venga aqui a sembrar las tierras!). Petra continues to excoriate the government for the inequities of the *quinta:* her son, who is married and has children, has to go, while someone else in the village who is single does not. The mayor responds that that is the government's affair. Finally, she bitterly condemns the practice of evading service through a cash payment. If everyone were treated equally, she could bear it, she says, but "the idea that a son should be killed, not necessarily because of the war, not necessarily because of the government, but because he is poor . . . You [*addressing the mayor*] don't understand because you don't have sons" (que le maten un hijo, quizás no por la guerra, ni por el gobierno, sino por la pobreza... Tú no te haces cargo porque no tienes hijos) (Millán 1899, 17). Although she is poor and cannot pay the commutation fee, while others who are well-off can—an egregious injustice—the mayor assures her that the government will give her son and every mother's son a hero's burial. She scoffs at this patently hypocritical assertion of governmental concern for the common soldier. The play's very title alludes to the government's callousness toward the poor. The fifteen soldiers are not even named in the newspaper report that bears the heading "Fifteen Casualties!" and records their anonymous deaths; only officers were listed by name in the press. Nor were relatives of fallen common soldiers officially notified of their deaths. Among Madrid papers only *El Heraldo de Madrid* made an effort to list the names of non-officers killed in battle (O'Connor 2001, 87). The play proceeds to illustrate further Petra's perception of the government's indifference.

The mother in this play is as resistant to the role assigned her by the government, that of making sacrifices—if need be, the sacrifice of a son—as mothers in other plays of the period, but unlike the others she is poor and voices the specific complaints of a mother who knows that she will now face even greater want. The mayor, the representative of authority in the play, simply dismisses her.[5]

A government that did not convincingly acknowledge the sacrifices of mothers and sons was at risk of losing the allegiance of the mass of the people. The Spanish government survived the risk, but in time the challenges to its discriminatory conscription policy by the real women of Zaragoza and elsewhere, as well as those on the stage and in popular fiction, helped to bring about the shift in national consciousness that the editorialist for *El Imparcial* referred to when he first learned of the women's request to demonstrate. That change, initially prompted by opposition to conscription and the war in Cuba, constituted a significant and unstoppable shift in the way many Spaniards viewed their country and its leaders. Eventually, in 1912, a new, nondiscriminatory conscription policy was adopted that allowed for no exemption fee or purchase of substitutes. In theory, at least, it put an end to the old inequities.[6]

# Conclusion

> We should bear in mind that although there was censorship on several occasions, the press laws that governed journalism from 1895 to 1910 granted all Spaniards "the right to freely express their ideas and opinions in speech or in writing, availing themselves of the press or any other similar means, without being subjected to prior censorship."
>
> MARÍA DEL CARMEN GARCÍA NIETO

In retrospect, the way in which the central event discussed in this essay was depicted in the press and elsewhere may be viewed as an instructive example of representation serving the same purpose as the ink of the squid. The manner in which the few women who actually participated in the 1896 demonstrations were made to function as straw men in order to set up correct versions of True Spanish Womanhood seems transparently obvious now as a strategy for avoiding sustained public discussion of the real issue at stake, the inequity of the *quinta* and the callous exploitation of the poor. While it is not possible to measure how or to what extent images of women and mothers—whether for or against conscription—influenced Spaniards' capacity to consider and evaluate the *quinta*, it is arguable that those who contributed, consciously or unconsciously, to a strategy of avoiding discussion did not fully succeed largely because the Spanish press in the 1890s, despite occasional attempts by the military and the government to impose censorship, nonetheless permitted expression of a wide range of information and opinion.

The class-based inequity of conscription was acknowledged on many occasions in the press and elsewhere. In his memoirs, Tomás Álvarez Ángulo (1962) recalled reports of the telling exchange between a delegation of workers who, in May 1896, asked the president of the Council of Ministers, Mateo Sagasta, to implement the legal obligation of all Spaniards to fight in wartime. Sagasta's response to their request was, "It is impossible to accede to your petition [. . .] because you yourselves must recognize that it would be an atrocity to house sons of good families in these terrible barracks we have" (Imposible acceder a la petición de ustedes [...] porque ustedes mismos reconocerán que sería una atrocidad llevar a los hijos de buenas familias a esos cuarteles tan malos que tenemos). The workers' representative responded to Sagasta's matter-of-fact reference to the economic, social, and cultural divide separating Spaniards by remarking that no one was demanding reforms—only compliance with the current law governing conscription in wartime.[1] In case his point was not taken, Álvarez Ángulo recalled a notice from about the same time published in *La Correspondencia de España*. The news item described a train wreck that had resulted in many dead and injured. "Fortunately, all the cars involved were third class" (Afortunadamente, todos los coches siniestrados eran de tercera clase) (181–82).

In its first number, of October 7, 1894, *La Lucha de Clases*, Spain's second oldest socialist paper after *El Socialista*, presented a vivid depiction of the miners in Vizcaya that strengthened the comparisons frequently made in those years between workers and slaves: "Never before have the conditions of slavery in the mining zone reached the point where they are today, to the extent that only the faces of the workers give the lie to the perception that these exploitations are located in Senegambia" (Nunca como hoy se ha llegado en la zona minera a un estado de esclavitud tal, que únicamente el rostro de los trabajadores desmiente que no se hallan estas explotaciones enclavadas en Senegambia) (Arbeloa 1970, 151–52). The paper went on to propose revolution as the only way to transform "this society of slaves" into one in which all men and women were equal.

The Spanish public that sought out information and critiques regarding conscription was clearly able to obtain it. Organizing to change the terms of military service was, nonetheless, beyond the capacity of anarchists, socialists, republicans, and others at the time, in part because of deeply rooted attitudes toward the working classes such as those Álvarez Ángulo illustrated and because slaverylike conditions for workers were widely tolerated. Women, like the working classes, were similarly undervalued, and their voices disregarded by the comfortable classes and by men. By the end of the century feminists and advocates of workers recognized that women and workers themselves would have to agitate for change in the way they were viewed and treated. Meanwhile, in the face of apparent impotence on the part of politically engaged men who urged reform, the women's march in Zaragoza was an uncomfortable anomaly, but one that had to be dealt with somehow both by supporters and by antagonists.

Although the women in Zaragoza did not overtly oppose the war in Cuba, the position of women vis-à-vis war quickly became the focus of discussion and commentaries on their action. Widespread speculation about the nature of women in relation to war and violence proved fruitful in the long run since it also led people to think about women in connection with suffrage, education, religion, and the law. In this sense the 1896 demonstration, embedded as it was in a rich context of dogma and opposing opinions and commentaries regarding women, helped to set the scene for the later entry of women into political life. It is particularly significant that women such as Rosario de Acuña, Soledad Gustavo, Teresa Claramunt, Àngeles López de Ayala, Belén Sárraga, and Carmen de Burgos, among others, contributed to the discussion by publishing opinions and expressing attitudes that contested the bromides of their bourgeois female counterparts. Except for Carmen de Burgos, they were marginal figures, but they struggled to make their voices heard in meetings, in plays, in pamphlets, and in the fifty or so anarchist newspapers that came and went between 1869 and 1898.[2]

In 1891 Teresa Claramunt wrote a letter in the "Section on Women" of the anarchist paper *El Combate* urging men to spur women on to the fight: "Onward, *compañeros*, propaganda, lots of propaganda, and above all propaganda directed to women, since you men can do little so long as women do not take an active part in revolutionary acts, but instead make their way to one or another disgusting confessional" (Adelante, pues, compañeros; propaganda, mucha propaganda, y, sobre todo, a la mujer, pues mientras la obrera no tome parte activa en los actos revolucionarios y, por el contrario, acuda al repugnante confesionario, poco podéis hacer los hombres) (Arbeloa 1970, 132). It is significant that Claramunt directly addressed men, not women, in her call to action. Before long, women themselves would take the initiative. Meanwhile, women such as those named above represented the unheard, small groups of women who read or had read to them anarchist papers and who attended anarchist, socialist, and republican meetings in cities, towns, and villages throughout Spain in the 1890s. Female dissidents made a difference for those women who listened to them, and they opened up what dialogue existed on meaningful issues to perspectives both men and women needed to take into account in the future.[3]

Finally, it is noteworthy that an image that would seem to rival that of weeping mothers or militant women in emotional potency—poor soldiers figured as black slaves—was seldom used for propaganda purposes during the war with Cuba. A reference to conscripts treated like slaves appeared in an article from *El Corsario* quoted above in chapter 2, in the section "Women Anarchists." The anarchist paper addressed the following words to the women of Zaragoza who had applied for permission to march in protest to the *quinta:* "Do you see, now that you are trying to protest those shipments worthy of slave traders in which the sons of workers are piled up like cargo, that any sign of protest is forbidden to you?"

The analogy was used with scathing irony by A. Ruiz Mateos in an article that appeared in *La Correspondencia Militar* on April 23, 1898, two days before the United States declared war on Spain. In the article, entitled "Obligatory Military Service" (El servicio militar obligatorio), the author noted:

> In the past year some eight thousand men have commuted their military service, and even supposing that they have all paid the 2,000 pesetas required for service outside the peninsula, they would have spent 16 million, though in fact the amount only comes to 14 million. The proletariat, on the other hand, has contributed one hundred thousand men

torn away from agriculture and industry, useful men all, and therefore we would not be exaggerating if we were to assign the same value to the lives of these men as that of an African slave—5,000 pesetas— although advanced nations value a slave's life at a higher rate. It would turn out then that the poor classes have contributed 500 million, . . . in a single year to the colonial wars.

En el año pasado han redimido su servicio de guerra próximamente unos 8,000 hombres, y aún suponiendo que todos lo hayan hecho a razón de 2,000 pesetas, como si fuera para Ultramar, resultarán 16 millones, aunque en verdad no llegan a catorce. El proletariado, en cambio, ha dado 100,000 hombres, arrancados a la agricultura y a la in-dustria, hombres útiles todos, y por tanto, no pecaremos de exagerados si tasamos la vida de uno de esos hombres en el mismo valor que la de un esclavo africano, en 5,000 pesetas, aunque las naciones adelantadas la aprecian en mucho más: resultaría, pues, que las clases pobres han contribuido con 500 millones,... en un solo año para las guerras colo-niales. (Hernández Sandoica and Mancebo 1978, 373)

Inhabitants of port cities where soldiers returning from Cuba were deposited knew at first hand what Blasco Ibáñez wrote concerning con-ditions on the voyage home: "Comillas [the Marqués de Comillas, head of the monopoly Transatlántica line] has collected millions of duros *ad majorem Dei gloriam* through his shipping business during this Cuban war, yet the transport of soldiers and sick men on his ships is carried out in the most inhumane manner imaginable. These voyages would have provided useful lessons to the former slavers of Guinea" (Co-millas lleva cobrados, *ad majorem Dei gloriam,* millones de duros por los transportes de la Guerra de Cuba, y sin embargo, las expediciones de soldados y enfermos son cargamentos inhumanamente realizados, que servirían de lección a los antiguos negreros de Guinea) (1978, 236).

In the late 1890s analogies drawn between soldier sons of the work-ing classes and slaves appear to have been as uncompelling and without consequence as the analogies drawn between slaves and women. Slav-ery had finally been abolished in Cuba only a decade earlier, and popu-lar attitudes toward blacks in Spain had not changed significantly from

earlier years, that is, negroes were considered biologically and cultur-
ally inferior to whites.[4] The entire weight of accepted scientific opinion supported the evolutionary inferiority of women, just as it affirmed
that of negroes. Women were characterized as "incomplete men" or
worse, while their cultural inferiority was apparent to everyone. A reviewer for *El Globo* (February 25, 1894) only half-spoofed contemporary
"scientific" studies on women in a review of Labadie-Lagrave's *Women's
Brains* (a book I have been unable to locate). Gloomy-minded scientists,
wrote the reviewer, "claim to discover in the brains of these enchanting
creatures the proof of their original inferiority. Some of them condemn
the most beautiful half of humanity to live in a state of irremediable incapacity; and if they do not dare to look upon their wives and daughters
as little chimpanzees, somewhat refined by civilization, they still consider them as children whose cerebral development will never be complete" (Pretenden hallar en el cerebro de este ser encantador la prueba
de su inferioridad original. Unos condenan la más hermosa mitad del
género humano a vivir en estado de incapacidad irremediable; y si no
se atreven a mirar a sus esposas e hijas como pequeños champancés,
algo refinados por un principio de civilización, las consideran cuando
menos como niños cuyo desarrollo cerebral nunca se completará).

The Spanish press, both liberal and conservative, presented a variety of reports concerning women in the mid and late 1890s, many of
them based on "scientific" studies similar in their conclusions to that
of Labadie-Lagrave. The prestigious literary and general cultural critic
Leopoldo Alas ("Clarín") contributed a series of "Readings" (Lecturas)
on the woman question in *La Ilustración Ibérica* beginning in 1894.
In his articles Alas took into account books and ideas on the subject
from a wide variety of mostly foreign writers. Alas believed in essential
differences between the sexes, and while he was careful to state that
sex differentiation did not imply value, he also noted that "according
to Darwin's theory, man is a continuation, a perfecting of woman, a
woman whose evolutionary process is ongoing" (Según la teoría de
Darwin, el hombre es una continuación, un perfeccionamiento de la
mujer; una mujer que acaba su evolución) (April 14, 1894). Alas contributed two articles titled "Nietzsche y las mujeres" (Nietzsche and

Women) to the Madrid paper *El Español* on September 6 and 7, 1899, in which women again figured as the inferior sex.[5]

How often during the 1890s and beyond did feminists and their sympathizers intone to little or no avail the hopeful mantra "Women must become the companions and not the slaves of men!" But invoking slavery as an evil was as likely to confound the public on the issues at stake as it was to persuade them to move in the desired direction. Workers were a class apart—nearly perceived as a race apart—and women were the inferior sex, thus making the analogy between workers and slaves, women and slaves more appropriate than objectionable in the eyes of many Spaniards.

Modest changes did come about in time; the 1896 demonstration and the commentaries to which it gave rise constituted a faltering but significant step toward changes in the perceptions of women and in their status in society. Above all, the 1896 demonstrations and the discussions they sparked afford us insights into the formidable obstacles—the Catholic Church, class and gender animosities—that blocked change, along with the beginnings of the meaningful struggle against them.

# Appendix

## The Seventeenth Century

### CATALINA DE ERAUSO, BORN CA. 1592

In the penultimate chapter of the autobiography attributed to Catalina de Erauso the author acknowledges her deception regarding her gender and, by implication, her violent ways but affirms her worth as a Spaniard who fought for the king and religion.

### ❧ Pasa de Génova a Roma ❧

Partí de Génova a Roma. Besé el pie a la Sanctitud de Urbano 8, referíle en breve, i lo mejor que supe, mi vida i corridas, mi sexo, i virginidad: i mostró Su Santidad extrañar tal caso i con afabilidad me concedió licencia para proseguir mi vida en hábito de hombre, encargándome la prosecución honesta en adelante, i la abstinencia en ofender al próximo, temiendo la ulción de Dios sobre su mandamiento, Non occides, i bolvíme.

Hízose el caso allí notorio, i fue notable al concurso de que me vide cercado de Personages, Príncipes, Obispos, Cardenales, i el lugar que me hallé abierto donde quería, de suerte que en mes i medio que estuve en Roma, fue raro el día en que no fuese combidado i regalado de Príncipes, i especialmente un Viernes fui combidado i regalado por unos Cavalleros, por orden particular i encargo del Senado Romano, i me asentaron en un libro por Ciudaddano Romano. Y día de San Pedro, 29 de Junio de 1626, me entraron en la Capilla de San Pedro donde vide los Cardenales con las ceremonias que se acostumbran aquel día. Y todos, o los más, me mostraron notable agrado i caricia, i me hablaron muchos. Y a la tarde, hallándome en rueda con tres Cardenales, me dixo uno de ellos, que fue el Cardenal Magalón, que no tenía más falta que ser Español, a lo qual le dixe:

—A mí me parece, señór, debajo de la corrección de Vuestra Señória Ilustrísisma q[u]e no tengo otra cosa buena.

........................

*I left Genoa for Rome, kissed the foot of His Holiness Urban VIII, and told him briefly, as well as I could, about my life, wanderings, sex, and virginity; and His Holiness was clearly amazed at my story and graciously gave me leave to go on wearing man's clothes, urging me to live uprightly in future, to avoid injuring my neighbor, and to fear God's vengeance respecting His commandment—*Non occides*. And then I withdrew.

My case became notorious in Rome, and [I] saw myself surrounded by a remarkable crowd of great personages—princes, bishops, and cardinals—and every door was thrown open to me; so that, during the month and a half that I spent in Rome, there was seldom a day that I was not invited and entertained by princes; and one Friday in particular, at the special order and expense of the Roman Senate, I was invited and entertained by certain gentlemen, and they inscribed my name on the roll as a Roman citizen. And on St. Peter's Day, June 29, 1626, they took me into the Chapel of St. Peter, where I saw the cardinals and the usual ceremonies of that feast-day; and all, or most of them, showed me every attention and kindness, and many of them conversed with me. And in the evening, while three cardinals were standing round me, one of them—it was Cardinal Magalon—said my only defect was that I was a Spaniard. To which I replied, "Speaking under correction, your Eminence, I think that is the only good thing about me."

Erauso 1992, 220, translation by James Fitzmaurice-Kelly

### The War of Independence, 1808–1814

#### LA CONDESA DE BURETA, 1775–1814

The following excerpt from the obituary notice published in a supplement to the *Gaceta de Zaragoza* on December 31, 1814, exalts the countess's valor and dedication during the French invasion.

---

* Unless otherwise indicated, translations are my own.

Alzado apenas un extremo del velo que cubría las nefandas tramas del más insidioso usurpador, estalló con tal vehemencia el fuego de su lealtad hacia nuestro adorado Fernando que bien lexos de asemejarse a aquellas centellas fosfóricas que despidieron en la misma época almas menos enérgicas que la suya, fue antes bien un volcán, que deborándola a ella mismo [sic] de continuo, arrebatada [sic] empós de sí a quantos la circuían.

Sus exhortos, sus donativos, sus tareas contribuyeron en gran parte a la heroica defensa de esta incomparable Capital: ni en aquellos días de horror y de gloria se limitó su intrépido zelo a restañar la sangre de su Compatriota herido, y a suministrar al defensor de la plaza todo género de armas y refrescos; en esta clase de servicios tubo un sin número de compañeras, más ella no contenta con esto trabaja infatigablemente en la construcción de baterias hasta encallecer sus manos, parapeta con sus mismos carruages las avenidas de la calle que habita en las violentas irrupciones del enemigo, y le espera allí a pie firme al frente de su vecindario.

Rendida Zaragoza, no se rinde su espíritu; marcha a las orillas del Cinca, y ciñe su sien con nuevos lauros en la espantosa rota que allí dieron nuestros Valientes a las más aguerridas tropas del Tirano. Manda este [sic] hacerle entonces mil ofertas, y las desecha todas con indignación; persiguenla [sic] con encarnizamiento, y huye de monte en monte, de pueblo en pueblo, sonriendo a las penalidades de la más desastrosa emigración: vuela a Reus, a Valencia, a Alicante, a Cádiz, y en este ultimo baluarte de nuestra independencia se manifiesta constantemente la misma, siempre fiel a su Rey, siempre amante a su Patria.

Ahuyentadas al Pirineo las águilas francesas, regresa a Zaragoza, y su casa es al momento el asilo del prisionero, el refugio del mendigo, el consuelo del patriota y el terror del infidente. Sí, su ardoroso zelo la hacía inexorable en varios lances, pero en llegar a cierto punto, siempre triunfaba su corazón. Ella era un astro benéfico y luminoso, que si padecía algún eclipse, era para aparecer más brillante y alhagüeño al tiempo de su emersion; y si en su fogosa carrera deslumbró con sus rayos al débil espectador, dulcificadados estos en su apacible ocaso, consolaron a quantos la vieron sumergirse tranquilamente en el océano de la eternidad para levantarse de nuevo hasta lo más excelso del Empíreo.

Tal conjunto de talante y de virtudes justamente mereció la singular

honra que le dispensó S.M. visitándola en su propia casa a su feliz trán-
sito por esta Ciudad, justamente merece el que su retrato se halle de
manifiesto en el Palacio Imperial de Petersburgo, y en la Real de Madrid,
y justamente merecerá el que la Madre España consigne en sus gloriosos
fastos la memoria de una Hija comparable por sus raras prendas con las
más célebres heroínas de la antigüedad.

---

A corner of the veil that concealed the odious schemes of that most in-
sidious usurper had scarcely been lifted when the ardor of her loyalty toward our adored Fernando burst out with such vehemence that far from
resembling those phosphorescent sparks that souls less energetic than
hers emitted at that time, hers was like a volcano, not only devouring her
continually but burning all those around her as well.

Her exhortations, her donations, the tasks she carried out, contributed in large part to the heroic defense of this incomparable Capital:
nor in those days filled with horror and glory did she limit her intrepid
zeal to staunching the blood of her wounded Compatriots and providing
the defenders of the town with all manner of arms and refreshments;
in this kind of service she was helped by innumerable female companions,
but not content with all this, she worked indefatigably in the building
of batteries until her hands were calloused, and with her own carriages
she barricaded the avenues of the street where she resided against the
violent attacks of the enemy and awaited him there, standing firm at
the head of the assembled residents.

Zaragoza having surrendered, her spirit did not surrender: she traveled
to the banks of the Cinca and girded her temples with fresh laurels during the frightful rout our Valiant soldiers dealt the most battle-hardened
troops of the Tyrant. The latter made her a thousand offers, and she rejected
them all with indignation; fiercely pursued, she fled from desert place to
desert place, from village to village, smiling in the face of the hardships
of such a disastrous emigration. She went to Reus, to Valencia, to Alicante,
to Cadiz, and in this last bastion of our independence she showed herself
always the same, always true to her King, always loving her Fatherland.

Once the French eagles had been pushed back to the Pyrenees, she returned to Zaragoza, where her house became the asylum of the prisoner, the refuge of the beggar, the consolation of the patriot, and the terror of those who had proved to be disloyal. Yes, her ardent zeal made her inexorable regarding several incidents, but when matters came to a certain point her heart always triumphed. She was a beneficent and luminous star that, if it suffered an eclipse now and then, only appeared brighter and more appealing when it emerged once again. And if in her ardent trajectory she dazzled the weak spectator with her rays, dimmed as they were in her peaceful decline, they served to console everyone who watched her sink tranquilly into the ocean of eternity in order to rise again to the heights of the Empyrean.

Such a union of talent and virtue justly merited the singular honor paid her by His Majesty when he visited her in her own house during his felicitous passage through this City. Just it was that her portrait should hang in the Imperial Palace of St. Petersburg and in the Royal Palace of Madrid. And she justly deserves the place that Mother Spain consigns to her in its glorious annals, that of a Daughter whose rare qualities make her comparable to the celebrated heroines of antiquity.

Blasco Ijazo, 1947, 20

## *The Nineteenth Century: The Education of Women*

### NICOLÁS SALMERÓN, 1838–1908

Salmerón was one of the presidents of the First Republic (1873), a Krausist, a professor of philosophy at the Universidad Central, and a tireless advocate of republicanism and of the separation of church and state in Spain. His views on women influenced the younger generation of Krausists, including Gumersindo de Azcárate and Leopoldo Alas.

❦ A lecture delivered on December 8, 1891 in the Centro Federal ❦

*In the English translation I have placed within brackets paraphrases of Spanish text that I have omitted.*

[...]

"En el problema de la educación está el gran secreto del perfeccionamiento humano," decía Kant, y una ley que la fisiología formula, establece que la degeneración, como el mejoramiento de la especie, se inicia siempre por el sexo femenino. De aquí la necesidad de reconocer 1a vital importancia de la educación de la mujer. Ya afirmaba Leibnitz que sería fácil reformar las instituciones sociales si se reformara la educación de la mujer y es también consideración de gran peso, aunque parezca inspirada en el egoismo de los hombres, la que expresaba Lheridan: las mujeres nos gobiernan; procuremos hacerlas perfectas.

[...]

El anatomista señala la diferencia, notable, entre la constitución orgánica del hombre y de la mujer. El desarrollo físico de ésta es incompleta; organizada para concebir y para la procreación de la especie, sus facultades activas distan mucho de igualar a las del hombre. El cerebro femenino tiene evolución más limitada y se asemeja al del niño; como en todo ser débil, el clima y otras condiciones naturales ejercen infuencia casi decisiva en la mujer. La precocidad de la mujer en los países cálidos y su ardimiento amoroso son bien conocidos. El celibato es contrario a la salud de la mujer; aquéllas que hacen voto de castidad, como las vestales de la Antigua Roma y las monjas de nuestro tiempo, las que en aras de la adoración religiosa consumen su vida en la oración y en el ayuno ascético, arrastran una vida miserable, martirizada por la clorosis y la histeria con que la naturaleza parece castigar la irracional privación del amor terrenal. Porque sólo el amor desarrolla la naturaleza feminina y abre a la luz su inteligencia. La solterona, la mujer que en el claustro siga postrada de hinojos fingiéndose quiméricas ilusiones de amor etéreo y celestial, son acaso las más desdichadas criaturas; se ceba en ellas la enfermedad, se vicia su naturaleza, y una muerte prematura es con frecuencia el desenlace fatal de un vida inútil. Es incalculable el perjuicio que las prácticas religiosas causan a las mujeres: hallan en su instinto de lo maravilloso, en su enfermiza imaginación soñadora, en su temperamento débil, terreno abonado, y hacen de ellas almas entregadas a la devoción, incapaces por eso mismo de sentir y practicar la verdadera piedad.

[…]

La mujer de los países civilizados es en nuestros tiempos un ser hipócrita, falso, que ama el lujo, la brillantez, lo artificial, lo extravagante, todo aquello que pugna con la razón y la verdad. Jamás se rinde ante las cualidades sólidas y positivas; busca el oropel y el bullicio; hace de la murmuración malévola e inconsistente su comidilla intelectual; se consume en la frivolidad y en la garrulería; adora, como dijo Goethe, las aventuras, y sobre todo, los aventureros; es un producto híbrido y artificial de la educación servil, que la hace creerse autómata destinado a obedecer a las supersticiones. "Cuando digo mujer," escribe Rabelais, "digo un sexo frágil, tan variable, mudable, inconstante e imperfecto, que la Naturaleza parece haberse apartado del buen sentido con que ha creado las demás cosas."

Los sucesos culminantes que han ejercido decisiva influencia en los destinos del hombre y han ayudado a su emancipación de ser racional—la creación de la familia, la constitución del Estado, el advenimiento del cristianismo y la Revolución francesa—no han modificado la naturaleza intelectual y moral de la mujer en proporción de los positivos progresos que en la historia de la humanidad aquellos sucesos han producido. Todo ser inteligente trabaja por su emancipación, y, como decía un ilustre autor inglés, todos los oprimidos inventan los medios de libertarse y de redimirse; la mujer no inventa nada, acepta de hecho su inferioridad con respecto al hombre, y fuera insano querer precipitar la obra de su redención, que sólo podrá conseguirse por un sistema adecuado de educación que transmitiéndose por acumulaciones hereditarias modifique su modo de ser y desarrolle sus aptitudes.

Es un error acreditado, y a que contribuyó la Revolución francesa, el de creer en la igualdad del hombre y de la mujer: no son iguales sus aptitudes ni sus energías; es diferente su misión social, que arranca de la diversidad de su naturaleza. En la lucha por la vida no puede pretender la mujer entablar rivalidad con el hombre; como ser más débil e inferior, sería aplastada en la concurrencia. Si se desconoce la naturaleza de la mujer, ha de ser peor el remedio y más infructuosos los resultados.

La constitución mental de la mujer es análoga a la de los hombres de las civilizaciones primitivas. La misma incapacided de raciocinio o de dejarse influir por él, la misma impotencia de atención y de reflexión, ausencia de espíritu de crítica, ineptitud para asociar las ideas y descubrir las relaciones y las diferencias, indecisión en las ideas, impotencia para dominar los reflejos, carácter impulsivo y facilidad para tomar por guía los instintos del momento.

Con estos elementos fácil es determinar la misión social de la mujer: la maternidad es la más alta; compañera del hombre, debe asociarse a su trabajos y preparar la vida de las generaciones futures y el mejoramiento de la especie. ¿Qué educación es la más propia para conseguirlo? Todos los progresos realizados se deben al libre pensamiento, a la filosofía y a la ciencia; se oponen a ellos la tradición y el ínterés.

Hoy recibimos hombres y mujeres tres clases de educación; la de nuestros padres, la universitaria en todos sus aspectos, dómine, preparaciones y exámenes, y la de la experiencia de la vida. Las dos primeras de nada sirven, o son, con harta frecuencia, perjudiciales. La de los padres es varia, y depende del grado de cultura y tolerancia de los progenitores; la universitaria es desastrosa; es una educación sin objeto, y es la que hace los caracteres sin fuerza. Como los seres orgánicos, las ideas tienen una larga evolución; son errores reonocidos por los espíritus superioress, y conservan todavía durante largo tiempo su prestigio entre las masas. Así ocurre con la educación encíclopédica e inconsistente de las universidades, sobre todo las Latinas. Se atiforra el entendimiento de múltiples y variadísimos conocimientos inútiles que se van arrinconando en la memoria; se trata de inculcar en la mollera del educando un diccionario enciclopédico que estaria mejor en la biblioteca, y en cambio nada se hace para despertar y desarrollar las cualidades que aseguran de hecho la superioridad de los individuos y de las razas: la iniciativa, la energía, el imperio de sí mismo, la precisión del razonamiento, la intimación rápida de las cosas. La Universidad no crea talentos superiores, ni inventores originales, ni pensadores profundos, ni escritores, ni políticos, ni hombres de ciencia. Galton, fisiólogo inglés, muestra en una notable estadística que los hombres eminentes de Inglaterra, en su mayoría, o no han recibido educación universitaria o han sido tristes alumnos que hacían exámenes poco brillantes, y se salían contínuamente de los programas. La vieja Universidad latina ha producido la actual burguesía con su débil sentido político, su falta de iniciativa, sus oscilaciones perpétuas de la rebeldía al despotismo, se escepticismo infecundo, su impotencia para sustentar la pesada carga de las creencias que exigen el sacrificio y el apostolado.

El objeto de la educación, según Renan, consiste en formar espíritus libres, juicios rectos y razonamientos seguros; es la verdadera preparación para la vida, que necesariamente, como dice Huxley, estriba en la instrucción científica, que habitúa el espíritu a la disciplina de la razón, poniéndole en contacto directo con los hechos; ejercitando la inteligencia en los procedimientos de la inducción e inculcando el amor al estudio, que es la observación constante de los fenómenos de la naturaleza y la investigación desinteresada de la verdad. Nada de esto consigue, antes bien entorpece e imposibilita la enseñanza universitaria esencialmente memorista, y más bien de forma que de fondo. Y en la mujer los efectos que produce esa desdichada tendencia a equpararla con el hombre son perniciosos; se hace de ella unas marisabidillas inconscientes, porque la mujer es incapaz de elevarse a las altas concepciones del espíritu; espíritus atiforrados de conocimientos superficiales, puramente memoristas, en que la historia, la geografía, y la literatura, se entrechocan y confunden, produciendo lamentable caos y perturbación en cerebros no muy resistentes; lo que es más sensible y doloroso, almas extraviadas y rebeldes, ignorantes de las prácticas de la vida, llenas de odio y amargura por el sentimiento de su inferioridad; y todo junto, la tensión cerebral constante, que no puede resistir su organismo, engendra en ellas gérmenes de raquitismo, que transmiten a las nuevas generaciones. Vale más, bajo el punto de vista social, una campesina robusta e ignorante que cualquiera de esas señoritas anémicas que frecuentan los salones, hablan francés, conocen al dedillo las innumerables batallas y la cronología de los reyes, bailan el rigodón, tocan el piano y se desmayan a cada paso.

La educación de la mujer debe inspirarse en la idea de hacer mujeres útiles que sean agradables. Hay que extirpar de la mujer la tendencia al fanatismo y arrancarla al yugo religioso, ennobleciendo las más humildes faenas domésticas, procurándolas una enseñanza moral que despierte el sentimiento de su responsabilidad social y de la utilidad de su misión en la familia; hay que inculcar en ellas el amor a la ciencia abandonándoles la enseñanza elemental, porque la analogía que existe entre el cerebro de la mujer y del niño las hace maravillosamente aptas a la educación de la primera infancia por el necesario nivel que debe establecerse entre el profesor que transmite los conocimientos y el educando que se los asimila, y otras varias profesiones sedentarias, como correos, administraciones comerciales, etc., para que las mujeres tienen indudablemente aptitud.

La enseñanza de la historia general de los descubrimientos científicos, poca literatura e historia sin genealogías de batallas, conocimientos profundos de higiene y terapéutica casera, derecho elemental porque han de ser esposas y madres de los ciudadanos, economía doméstica, trabajos femeninos, para lo cual son de gran utilidad las escuelas profesionales, artes semi-manuales, como los de la costura, porque precisa arrancarlos a la depuración de la promiscuidad del taller, algunos conocimientos de lujo, música y pintura, tales debieran ser las materias que abarcase la instrucción de la mujer.

El Estado, que algo se preocupa por la educación del hombre, permanece indiferente ante la de la mujer, y ya decía Montesquieu que la buena educación nace de las buenas leyes. Sólo una forma de Gobierno científica, la república democrática, puede procurer la verdadera emancipación de la mujer, condicionándola para el cumplimiento de su misión en la vida: ser la inteligente compañera del hombre y hacer las generaciones futuras vigorosas de cuerpo, sanas de alma, aptas para la vida.

..................

[Salmerón begins by avowing his inability to deal adequately with the subject.]

Kant wrote that "the secret of human perfectibility lies in the problem of education," and one of the laws of physiology establishes that the degeneration as well as the betterment of the species is always initiated by the female sex. Hence the need to recognize the vital importance of the education of women. Leibnitz affirmed that it would be easy to reform social institutions if women's education were reformed, and Lheridan's statement that "women govern us; let us try to make them perfect," although it may seem inspired by male egoism, is also worthy of consideration.

[Salmerón proposes to apply the method of positive observation in the development of the topic of his lecture: women and education. First, he will discuss female physiology and the social condition of women in order to determine their mental capabilities and the function they are called upon to serve in life. Then, by defining the object of education in general, he will establish the system that is best suited to the faculties and aptitudes of women and to the fulfillment of their social mission in life.]

The anatomist points out the difference—and it is a notable one—between the organic constitutions of men and women. The physical development of the latter is incomplete; organized in order to conceive and procreate the race, women's active faculties are far from equaling those of men. The female brain has evolved in a more limited way and resembles the brain of a child. As in every weak being, climate and other natural conditions exercise an influence on women that is almost decisive. The precocious development of women in hot climates and their ardently amorous nature are well known. Celibacy is bad for a woman's health; those who take a vow of chastity, like the vestal virgins of ancient Rome and the nuns of our times, those who in the service of religious adoration consume their lives in ascetic prayer and fasting, drag on miserable lives, martyred by the chlorosis and hysteria with which nature punishes the irrational deprivation of earthly love. For love alone develops a woman's nature and opens her intelligence to the light. The celibate woman, the woman who kneels prostrated in the cloister constructing for herself chimerical illusions of ethereal, celestial love, is perhaps the most wretched of creatures; illness feeds on her, her physical nature is vitiated, and a premature death is often the fatal outcome of her useless life. The harm religious practices cause in women is incalculable: those practices find fertile terrain in women's instinct for the marvelous, their sickly, dreamy imaginations, their weak temperament; and these practices make of them souls delivered over to devotion, incapable on their own of feeling and practicing genuine piety.

[Salmerón proceeds to state that marriage is more necessary for women than for men and leads to true chastity, although the institution has degenerated in modern civilizations to become little more than an economic contract or a union forged by caprice.]

In our time women in civilized countries are false, hypocritical creatures who love luxury; they love what is brilliant, artificial, extravagant—everything that is at odds with reason and truth. Women never bow before solid and positive qualities. They seek glitter and commotion; they make malevolent and insubstantial gossip their intellectual fodder; they are consumed with frivolity and chatter; as Goethe said, they love adventures and, above all, adventurers. Women are the hybrid and artificial product of a servile education, which makes them believe that they are automatons destined to obey superstitions. "When I say woman," Rabelais wrote, "I refer to a fragile sex, so variable, mutable, inconstant, and imperfect that Nature seems to have strayed from the good sense that guided the rest of creation."

The culminating events that have exercised a decisive influence on the destinies of men and have contributed to their emancipation as rational beings—the creation of the family, the constitution of the state, the advent of Christianity, and the French Revolution—have not modified the intellectual and moral nature of women in the direction of positive progress, as has otherwise occurred in the history of humanity. All intelligent beings work toward emancipation, and as an illustrious English writer wrote, all oppressed beings invent ways to liberate and redeem themselves, but not women, who invent nothing and who accept their inferiority with respect to men. It would be madness to try to hasten the work of their redemption. It can only be achieved by means of a proper education, which, transmitting its gains by hereditary accumulation, will modify their mode of being and develop their aptitudes.

The French Revolution contributed to the erroneous idea that men and women are equal. They are not equal either in their aptitudes or in their energies. Their social missions, which derive from their different natures, are different. Since women are weaker and inferior, they cannot compete with men in the struggle for life. If one does not understand women's nature, the remedy will be worse than the ailment, and the results fruitless.

The mental constitution of women is analogous to that of men in primitive civilizations. Women evince the same incapacity for reasoning or being influenced by reason, an inability to focus attention and to reflect, an ineptitude for associating ideas and uncovering relationships and differences, indecision, an inability to master conditioned reflexes, an impulsive character, and a tendency to follow instinct as dictated by the moment.

It is easy with the foregoing in mind to determine the social mission of women: maternity is the highest mission; as the companion of a man, a woman ought to join him in his endeavors and prepare the life of future generations and the betterment of the species. What kind of education is best suited to achieve these goals? All progress is owing to free inquiry, to philosophy, and to science. Tradition and special interests are opposed to progress.

Today men and women receive three kinds of education: what we learn from our parents; what we learn from the university in all its aspects, the teacher, study, and examinations; and what we learn from life itself. The first two are not good for anything or are, often enough, harmful. Education provided by parents varies and depends on the degree of culture and tolerance possessed by one's progenitors. University education is disastrous; it is an education without an object, and it is what forms individuals lacking in a forceful character. Like organic beings, ideas have a long evolution; their errors are recognized by superior minds, but they preserve their prestige among the masses for a long time. This is what happens with the encyclopedic and insubstantial education provided by universities, above all by Latin universities. One's mind is stuffed with multiple, extremely varied, useless knowledge, which is stored away in corners of the brain; an attempt is made to place an entire encyclopedic dictionary in the student's head, but nothing is done to awaken and develop the qualities that in reality ensure the superiority of individuals and races: initiative, energy, self-mastery, precise reasoning, a rapid grasp of matters. The university does not create superior talents, or original inventors, or profound thinkers, or writers, or politicians, or men of science. Galton, an English physiologist, has demonstrated with statistics worthy of note that the majority of the eminent men of England either did not receive a university education or were indifferent students who wrote undistinguished exams and departed often from the required courses of study. The old Latin University has produced the present bourgeoisie, with its weak political sense, its lack of initiative, its perpetual oscillations from rebellion to despotism, its sterile skepticism, its inability to sustain the heavy weight of beliefs that demand sacrifice and a true calling.

The object of education, according to Renan, is to form unfettered minds, upright judgment, and solid reasoning. It is the true preparation for life, which necessarily, as Huxley says, stems from a scientific education, which habituates the mind to the discipline of reason by placing it in direct contact with facts, by exercising the intelligence in the processes of induction, and by inculcating a love for study that amounts to the constant observation of natural phenomena and the disinterested investigation of truth. None of this is attained—rather it is dulled and made impossible—by a university education based on memorization, an education characterized by form and not content. The effects on women of the unfortunate tendency to equate them with men are pernicious. It makes them into unwitting bluestockings because they are incapable of reaching the higher realms of conceptualization; their minds are stuffed with superficial knowledge learned by rote, in which history, geography, and literature bump up against each other and become confused. All this produces a lamentable chaos and perturbation in minds that are not able to cope with disorder. What is most hurtful and painful in such an education is that it produces wayward and rebellious souls, women who are ignorant of the normal practices of life, women filled with hatred and bitterness over their sense of inferiority, and, above all, women who experience a constant cerebral tension, which their organism cannot resist, engendering in them the seeds of stunted development, which they pass on to future generations. From the point of view of society's welfare, a robust and ignorant country girl is worth more than any one of these anemic young ladies who frequent salons, speak French, know by heart innumerable battles and kings, dance the rigadoon, play the piano, and faint at the drop of a hat.

The education of women ought to be inspired by the idea of producing useful women who are also agreeable. It is necessary to extirpate their tendency to fanaticism and to remove the yoke of religion from them by ennobling the humblest domestic tasks, providing them with a moral education that will awaken in them a sense of social responsibility and of the utility of their mission in the family. A love of science must be instilled in women, and they should be the educators of elementary-school children. The analogy that exists between the brains of women and children makes them marvelously well suited for teaching children because of the necessary common level that must be established between the educator, who transmits knowledge, and the child, who assimilates it. Other varied, sedentary professions, such as the postal service, commercial administrations, etc., are professions for which women undoubtedly have an aptitude.

Subjects that women ought to study include the general history of scientific discoveries; very little literature; history without the genealogies of battles; extensive information pertaining to hygiene and domestic medicine; elementary law, since women are to be wives and mothers of citizens; home economics; trades suitable for women, for which there is training at professional schools; semi-manual arts such as sewing, because it is necessary to draw women away from the promiscuity of the dressmaker's shop; and a few luxury accomplishments, such as music and painting.

The State, which takes some interest in the education of men, remains indifferent to the education of women. Montesquieu said some time ago that a good education derives from good laws. Only a form of government that is scientific, only a democratic republic, can bring about the true emancipation of women by conditioning them for the fulfillment of their mission in life, which is to be the intelligent companion of men and to form future generations that will be fit for life, sound in body, with healthy minds.

*El Nuevo Régimen,* December 12, 1891

\* \* \*

## The Nineteenth Century: Women and Science

### ODÓN DE BUEN Y DEL COS, 1863–1945

Professor of natural history at the University of Barcelona from 1889 until 1895, when he was temporarily removed from his position because of his Darwinist views (his textbooks were placed on the Index by the Catholic Church). Suspected of complicity in the events of the Tragic Week in Barcelona (1909), he was excommunicated by the bishop of Barcelona and forced to move to Madrid, where he assumed a chair as professor of natural history in 1911. He was jailed in Mallorca at the outset of the Civil War and later went into exile in Mexico. He was one of the preeminent founders of the science of oceanography in Spain and an outspoken advocate of socialism, republicanism, and rights for women.

[...]

Escribiendo este artículo trabajo, pero conmemoro la fiesta del 1.0 de Mayo; y la conmemoro uniendo mi pensamiento al de los trabajadores todos que hoy se agitan en busca del bienestar que esta sociedad caduca les niega; la celebro dedicando mi labor a *la mujer*, inspirado en las líneas del librito de Cristóbal Litrán. ¡Qué mejor conmemoración! Sufre el obrero la tiránica imposición del capital monopolizado por la ignorancia o por el egoismo, sufre las imposiciones de gobiernos autoritarios, es aún súbdito en vez de ser átomo de autoridad social, pero sus vejámenes no tienen punto de comparación con aquellos de que la mujer es víctima.

La tradición ha formado, y las leyes y costumbres sostienen, ese medio inicuo en que la mujer vive aun en nuestro tiempo, ese convencionalismo tiránico que si rodea, en la apariencia de dignidad y de poesía a las madres de los hombres, elevándolas por el sentimiento, las esclaviza como mujeres, negándoles el desenvolvimiento de la inteligencia y erigiendo al propio tirano, al hombre, en defensor y representante. El problema social tiene trascendencia e importancia por lo que al hombre se refiere; es verdad que pugna con la cultura presente el que no halle garantido *de hecho* el derecho a la vida; es verdad que las deducciones científicas aun no son patrimonio de todos; pero no deja de ser también cierto que las conquistas políticas dan el poder al ciudadano, y que éste, adquiriendo y ejerciendo el derecho de ciudadanía, es a la vez agente del progreso social y partícipe de sus ventajas.

Pero ¿y la mujer? ¿Es agente social en la medida que su condición racional le permite? ¿Tiene en sus manos el derecho de redimirse, o está bajo tutela, apareciendo incapacitada de influir con su razón y por su derecho en el concierto social?

¡La mujer! ¡Qué hermosa misión la suya y a qué triste condición no queda reducida! Cuántas veces mientras el padre, el esposo, el hijo, o el hermano, luchan en el palenque de la razón o luchan en la barricada por redimir al que trabaja y conquistar para el mañana la armonía y el bienestar social que ellos no disfrutan y que, en cambio de los esfuerzos generosos de hoy han de disfrutar mañana nuestros hijos, cuántas veces al sacrificarse por la más grande de las empresas humanas, les amarga la idea de que allá en un rincón de su casa llora la hija, la esposa, la madre o la hermana, por no comprender lo que aquel sacrificio significa, que de comprenderlo ¿qué corazón de mujer había de resistir a prestar su concurso a obra tan generosa y tan humana? ¿No es verdad que si la mujer comprendiera el alcance de la lucha social, en vez de amargar con sus lágrimas la senda del que lucha, la llenaría de flores?

Entienda la hermosa mitad del género humano que aquel hombre que lucha desinteresado por la solución del problema social no lucha por él solo, lucha también por la mujer cuya redención es aun más preciosa que la del hombre, lucha sobre todo más que por la actual generación, por la que han de formar nuestras hijas y nuestros hijos.

Pero entiendan también los obreros que su campaña será incompleta y además egoista, si no luchan por redimir a la mujer con más urgencia y más energía si cabe, que por la propia redención. Y para llegar a un resultado favorable en tal empeño, pidan ante todo que a la mujer se le ilustre se le eduque, no bajo la pesada losa de los convencionalismos tradicionales, sino con la amplia base que, inspirada en la Ciencia positiva, la pedagogía moderna pone en práctica.

❈❈❈

Hay quien afirma que la mujer no llega al alcance intelectual del hombre, que en su cerebro se nota cierta inferioridad demostrada por la Antropología, que su organización es un obstáculo para el cumplimiento de los altos fines de la inteligencia, que no puede, ni debe tener derechos políticos, ni le alcanzan los deberes sociales que el hombre está llamado a cumplir. Veamos el fundamento científico de tales afirmaciones.

¿Quién negará la capacidad de la mujer para el cultivo de la Ciencia y del Arte? Ante los hechos hay que inclinar la cabeza; conocemos mujeres que han inmortalizado su nombre en la Literatura, en la Filosofía, en las Ciencias positivas; luego la mujer es apta para los labores del pensamiento. Y no cabe decir que aquellos casos son excepcionales; si un organismo llega a realizar una funcion determinda, hay que reconcer *de hecho* que ningún obstáculo tiene la organización aquella para el desempeño de la función realizada.

Es cierto que en las estadísticas antropométricas, la mujer sale perjudicada con relación al hombre; todos los caracteres muestran menor capacidad intelectual, pero ninguno falta de aptitud; todas las señales de degeneración de los tipos humanos se manifiestan preferentemente y en proporción mayor en la mujer que en el hombre.

Tras del reconocimiento de estos hechos es necesario contestar a la siguiente pregunta: la menor capacidad, la mayor tendencia a la degeneración, ¿son debidas a imposiciones orgánicas irremediables, o son, por el contrario, un efecto de la diferente manera con que la sociedad ha considerado a la mujer que al hombre? Y planteada así la cuestión ¿osará alguien, en nombre de la Ciencia, afirmar que en el organismo de la mujer hay disposiciones que imposibilitan una educación científica, racional, hasta alcanzar el mismo nivel de hombre?

No, no tiene la admirable organización de nuestra hermosa compañera nada que rebaje su condición racional, nada que se oponga al desenvolvimiento de las facultades psíquicas; no hay señales que denoten falta de aptitudes intelectuales; si alguna inferioridad muestra el cerebro aprisionado en esas cabezas divinamente formadas, de líneas perfectas y de proporciones armónicas, no es obra de la Naturaleza, es obra de la irracional educación que a la mujer se ha dado, del brutal concepto en que las sociedades le tuvieron siempre.

El cerebro, como todos los órganos, las funciones psíquicas, como todas las demás del organismo, se amoldan al medio, se perfeccionan gradualmente. La mujer ha vivido y vive en medio distinto que el hombre; a la mujer se le ha educado de un modo diferente; ésta es la causa de las diferencias que los cerebros presentan y los cráneos reflejan al ser concienzudamente observados.

Y ningún agente ha influído tanto en la degeneración intelectual de la mujer como la educación religiosa; ésta, con sus tendencies al misticismo, con el abuso de la fantasia que se ceba en los organismos débiles, debilitándolos aun más; al señalar como estado perfecto el que huye de la Naturaleza y se entrega a un sobrenaturalismo aterrador unas veces, placentero otras, contrario a la higene mental siempre, ha impreso al organismo femenino el sello de la neurosis y ha hecho a la histérica el tipo dominante y dominador en una sociedad católica y por añadidura meridional.

Las mismas aptitudes que nuestras mujeres muestran; su carácter dado a la fantasia, más que a la razón; el sentimiento, en casos sublime, en casos grosero, que suele ser la norma de sus acciones, son pruebas de un desnivel mental, hijo de una educación defectuosa.

En pueblos que no tienen la tradición católica del nuestro, la mujer no brilla en el mundo de las letras cultivando especialmente la literatura mística o el sentimentalismo aplicado a cualquier manifestación de la vida, pero, en cambio, ayuda al hombre en la investigación científica, cultiva las ciencias físicas y naturales, poniendo de relieve que para la observación de la Naturaleza, para depurar hasta la minuciosidad los hechos o describir detalladamente los seres, no sólo tiene la facilidad del hombre, sino que le aventaja en muchos casos.

Aparte la aptitud para las más altas labores del pensamiento, perfectamente demostrada, sabidas son las que muestra la mujer para los trabajos administrativos. Las casas de comercio que tienen confiados sus libros, la venta, recepción y clasificación de géneros o cualquier otra faena análoga, y hasta la dirección de importantes negocios a las mujeres, saben bien con cuanta facilidad cumplen éstas la misión que se les confía. Alguna sociedad conozco yo, cuya secretaría, dirigida por una señorita, puede servir de ejemplo a las de muchos establecimientos públicos, por el método y por la acertada distribución del trabajo.

Ahora bien: ¿debe la mujer tener derechos políticos? ¿está capaci-
tada para ejercer la función social del ciudadano en las democracias? Si
la Naturaleza le ha dado aptitud intelectual y la educación le capacita
para las elevadas funciones del pensamiento; si la mujer puede, como
Doña Concepción Arenal—la ilustre pensadora, de robusta cultura y
sólido juicio, cuyos trabajos llamaron la atención de los jurisconsul-
tos en el último Congreso de San Petersburgo,—si puede interpreter el
derecho en sus más altas aplicaciones, ¿cómo no ha de poder ejercer el
más rudimentario de los derechos, el que se considera indiscutible, el
que deriva del reconocimiento de la personalidad racional?

¿Tiene la mujer individualidad social? ¿Está capacitado para las
funciones que el reconocimiento de la individualidad trae consigo? Si
lo está, deben concedérsele los derechos individuales. Si no lo está,
demostrado queda que no es por obra de la sociedad misma; debe ésta
subsanar el error mediante la educación.

En el Estado, con cuya racional organización los socialistas inten-
tamos remediar las desigualdades del presente, teniendo por norma el
cumplimiento de la Justicia en la sociedad humana, la mujer recobrará
la individualidad a que tiene derecho; en la República, que se considera como el medio en que la transformación social ha de realizarse de
un modo sólido, el problema de la educación de la mujer será de los
resueltos en primer término; porque lo sea y porque, huyendo del misticismo y del dogma, se inspire en la Ciencia positiva, hemos de luchar
sin descanso los que estamos convencidos de la influencia que la mujer
tiene *de hecho* en el régimen de la sociedad y tendrá en la dirección de
las generaciones venideras.

Y con las líneas trazadas doy por cumplido el encargo de preparar
al lector para que lea este librito y quede convencido del juicio que a
los hombres del catolicismo mereció la personalidad de la mujer, tan
respetada y tan dignificada por el socialismo.

....................

[Odón explains that, constrained by his work schedule, he is writing
the prologue to Litrán's book on May 1 while other workers and their
advocates are celebrating.]

I am working as I write this article, but I am commemorating the May 1 festival, and I commemorate it by uniting my thought to that of all the workers who are bestirring themselves today in search of the well-being that this dying society denies them; I celebrate the festival by dedicating my labor to *women*, inspired by Cristóbal Litrán's little book. What better commemoration! The worker suffers the tyrannical imposition of capital monopolized by ignorance or by greed, he suffers the impositions of authoritarian governments, he is still a subject rather than an atom of social authority, but his humiliations do not compare at all to the humiliations that victimize women.

The iniquitous environment in which women live even in our day has been formed by tradition and upheld by laws and customs. This tyrannical conventionalism in appearance surrounds the mothers of men with dignity and poetry, elevating them by means of sentiment, but in reality it enslaves them as women, denying them the development of their intelligence and at the same time setting up men as their defenders and representatives.

The social problem has transcendence and importance as far as men are concerned; it is true that the man who does not *in fact* have his right to life guaranteed struggles against the present culture; it is true that scientific deductions are not yet the patrimony of all; but it is no less true that political conquests give power to the citizen and that by acquiring and exercising the right to citizenship he is at one and the same time an agent of social progress and a participant in its advantages.

But women? Are they social agents to the degree that their condition as rational beings permits? Do they hold in their own hands the right to redeem themselves, or are they under tutelage, apparently unable to influence the social body with their reason and in accord with their rights?

Women! What a beautiful mission is theirs and to what a wretched state they have been reduced! How many times while the father, husband, son, or brother struggles in the stockade of reason or fights on the barricades in order to redeem workingmen and conquer for the future the harmony and social well-being that they do not enjoy and that, on the other hand, our sons and daughters are to enjoy tomorrow, in exchange for our generous efforts—how many times, as men sacrifice themselves for the greatest of human endeavors, are they not embittered by the idea that there, in a corner of the house, a daughter, wife, mother, or sister sits weeping because she cannot understand what that sacrifice means, for if she did understand, what woman's heart would resist lending her help to such a generous and humane work? Is it not true that if women understood the implications of the social struggle, instead of embittering with their tears the path on which men fight, they would cover it with flowers?

Let the beautiful half of the human race understand that the man who fights disinterestedly on behalf of the solution to the social problem does not fight for himself alone. He fights also for women, whose redemption is even more precious than that of men. He fights above all, more than for the present generation, for the generation to be formed by our daughters and sons.

But let workers understand also that their campaign will be incomplete and egoistic as well if they do not fight to redeem women with more urgency and greater energy, if that is possible, than for their own redemption. And in order to attain a favorable outcome in such an endeavor, let them ask above all that women become enlightened and educated, not under the heavy weight of tradition and convention, but rather upon the broad base that modern pedagogy puts into practice, inspired by positivistic science.

❦

There are those who affirm that women do not attain the intellectual level of men, that Anthropology demonstrates that their brains are inferior, that their organization constitutes an obstacle to the fulfillment of the lofty aims of the intellect, that they cannot, nor should they, have political rights, nor are they called upon to comply with the social obligations assumed by men. Let us examine the scientific foundation of such affirmations.

Who will deny the capacity of women for the cultivation of Science and Art? One must bow one's head before the facts: we know women who have immortalized their names in Literature, in Philosophy, in the positive sciences; therefore, women possess an aptitude for intellectual work. And it is not correct to state that those cases are exceptional; if an organism comes to fulfill a particular function, it must be recognized *in fact* that there is no obstacle preventing that organism from carrying out the function it has fulfilled.

It is true that in regard to anthropometric statistics women come out worse than men; all the measurable factors demonstrate less intellectual capacity but no lack of aptitude; all the signs of degeneration in human types manifest themselves preferentially and in greater proportion in women than in men.

After recognizing these facts, it is necessary to answer the following question: is their lesser capacity and greater tendency to degeneration owing to irremediable organic dispositions, or are these dispositions, on the contrary, an effect of the different ways women and men have been treated by society? And when the question is posed in this fashion, can anyone, in the name of Science, dare to affirm that there are dispositions in the organism of women that rule out a scientific, rational education that would allow them to reach the same level as men?

No, the admirable organization of our beautiful companion reveals nothing that downgrades her capacity for reason, nothing that opposes the development of her mental faculties; there are no signs that denote a lack of intellectual aptitude. If the brain imprisoned in those divinely formed feminine heads, with perfect lines and harmonic proportions, shows any inferiority, it is not the work of Nature but the consequence of the irrational education given to women, the result of the brutal concept society has always held of them.

The brain, like all the organs, mental functions, like all the rest of the functions in the organism, mold themselves to the environment and gradually perfect themselves. Women have lived, and still live, in an environment that is different from that of men. Women have been educated differently. This is the cause of the differences presented by their brains and their craniums when they are conscientiously observed.

And no agent has exerted as much influence on the intellectual degeneration of women as religious education. Women, with their tendency toward mysticism, with their abuse of fantasy, which feeds on weak organisms, weakening them even more, are prey to religion, which considers perfect the state of those who flee from Nature and deliver themselves over to a supernaturalism that is terrifying sometimes and pleasing at other times, but which is always contrary to mental hygiene—religion has impressed the stamp of neurosis on the female organism and has made the hysteric the dominant and dominating type in a society that is Catholic and meridional to boot.

The very aptitudes that our women demonstrate; their character given to fantasy rather than to reason, their capacity for feeling—sometimes sublime and sometimes gross—which usually guides their actions, are together proof of a mental disparity, the result of a defective education.

In countries without our Catholic tradition women do not excel in the world of letters by cultivating mystic literature or a sentimentalism applied to any and all manifestations of life. Rather, they help men in scientific research, they cultivate the physical and natural sciences, revealing in the process that in the observation of Nature, when it comes to the minute observation of facts or the description of entities in detail, not only do women possess the same facility as men but they outperform them in many instances.

Apart from a demonstrable aptitude for the highest levels of thought, the aptitude women show for administrative tasks is well known. Houses of commerce that entrust to women their account books, the sale, reception, and classification of fabrics, or some other analogous task, even the direction of important negotiations, know well with what ease women fulfill the missions entrusted to them. I know a company whose administrative department, led by a woman, can serve as an example to those of many public establishments because of its methods and delegation of work.

Should women have political rights? Are they suited to exercise the social function of citizens in a democracy? If Nature has provided them with the intellectual aptitude, and education enables them to carry out the elevated functions of thought, if women can, like Doña Concepción Arenal—the illustrious thinker with a robust culture and solid judgment, whose work caught the attention of judges in the last

Congress in St. Petersburg—if women can interpret the law in its highest applications, why should they not be capable of exercising the most rudimentary of rights, the one that is considered indisputable, the one that derives from the recognition of the rational personality?

Does a woman possess social individuality? Is she capable of performing functions that the recognition of individuality entails? If she is, then individual rights ought to be conceded to her. If not, then it has been demonstrated that it is not due to Nature, but rather it is the work of society itself, and society must rectify its error by means of education.

In the State, through whose rational organization we socialists are trying to remedy the inequalities of the present time, holding as the norm the fulfillment of Justice in human society, woman will recover the individuality she is entitled to; in the Republic, which is deemed the environment where the social transformation will take place in a solid manner, the problem of women's education will be one of the first to be resolved. Those of us who are convinced of the influence that women have *in fact* in the conduct of society and the influence they will have in future society will fight tirelessly to resolve the problem of education, fleeing from mysticism and dogma and inspired by positivist science.

And with these lines I consider that I have discharged the task of preparing the reader so that he may read this book and be made fully aware of the judgment passed down on women by men of the Catholic faith—on the personhood of women, which is so highly respected and so dignified by the tenets of socialism.

Buen 1892


*The Nineteenth Century: Women in the Public Sphere?*
*A Modest Demur*

### MARÍA DEL PILAR SINUÉS, 1835–1893

The author of novels and articles published in magazines and newspapers widely read in Spain and Latin America, María del Pilar Sinués was a determined advocate of training women to become angels of the hearth and home.

✖ "Una carta de D.a María del Pilar Sinués" ✖

Sr. D. Mariano de Cavia

Distinguido señor de toda mi consideración:

He leído ayer 11 en *El Liberal* el artículo de usted condenando con su gracia e ingenio acostumbrado, la idea de que las señoras puedan ser socias del Ateneo; yo quiero sincerarme, mi estimado Señor, de la parte que me pudiera atribuir—siquiera de pensamiento—en sus Justas censuras, porque lejos de querer penetrar en esos centros hechos y formados para que brille el talento del hombre he rehusado siempre, con el temor propio de quien nada vale, toda publicidad; he escrito libros y sigo escribiéndolos, como único elemento de vida, y porque el cielo me ha privado de todos los demás; yo no he hecho competencia a nadie, ni he deseado más Gloria que ser la amiga del hogar; sólo he procurado en mis libros que el alma de la mujer viva en una atmósfera de luz, de paz y de fuerza cristianas; la he conducido al dulce país del ideal, y en él la he enseñado lo que sé únicamente; que no hay en la humanidad más que una ley que nos salve y nos guíe: la ley del amor y de la caridad; que no hay otra sabiduría—ni la necesitamos—que el saber de memoria el Código sublime que nos dejó el divino ajusticiado del Gólgota, y que nos manda sufrir, amar y perdonar.

Ya ve usted, mi estimado señor, que sabiendo tan poco, no puedo ser incluída entre las marisabidillas. Jamás he tenido el honor de pisar el Ateneo, ni aún para ir a la tribuna pública a escuchar a las eminencies de mi sexo; y aunque todas las señoras de Madrid se hicieran socias de aquel docto centro, yo no lo sería jamás; admiro en las reseñas de los periódicos cuanto bueno se lee allí, pero mejor que en ninguna parte me encuentro en mi casa, de la que apenas salgo, partiendo las horas de la velada entre un bordado o costura, la lectura de algún libro muy sencillo y la plegaria al cielo por las almas de los seres que me fueron queridos.

En tan poco estimo la publicidad que nunca nombran mis libros los periódicos y, sin embargo, sólo de su producto vive su muy atenta y S.S. y paisana,

q.b.s.m.,

María del Pilar Sinués

12 abril, 1892

### ❧ A letter by D.a María del Pilar Sinués ❧

Sr. D. Mariano de Cavia

Distinguished sir worthy of my most sincere consideration:

Yesterday, the 11th, I read your article in *El Liberal* condemning with your customary wit and ingenuity the idea that women could be members of the Athenaeum. I want to be sincere, my dear sir, about any role that might be attributed to me—even in thought—regarding your Just censure, because far from wishing to penetrate into those centers, made and formed in order that the talent of men might shine within, I have always declined all publicity owing to the trepidation natural to one who is quite unworthy. I have written books, and I continue to write them, as the only means of earning my livelihood and because Providence has deprived me of all other means of doing so. I have not entered into competition with anyone, nor have I desired any Glory other than that of friend of the hearth. In my books I have sought only to enable a woman's soul to live in an atmosphere of light, of peace, and of Christian fortitude. I have led her into the sweet country of the ideal, and once there, I have taught her the only thing I know, that there is one law in humanity that saves and guides us: the law of love and charity; that there is no other wisdom—nor do we have need of it—than knowing by heart the sublime Code, which the divine victim of Golgotha bequeathed us and which commands us to suffer, to love, and to pardon.

Now you can see, my dear sir, that knowing so little, I cannot be included among the bluestockings. I have never had the honor of crossing the threshold of the Athenaeum, not even in order to attend the public tribunal to hear eminent speakers of my own sex. And even were all the ladies in Madrid to become members of that learned center, I would never do so. I admire all the fine things I read about it in newspaper reviews, but better than anywhere else I am suited to my house, from which I seldom venture, dividing the evening hours between embroidery or sewing, the reading of some simple book, and prayers to heaven on behalf of the souls of those whom I have loved.

So little do I esteem publicity that newspapers never mention my books, and yet from their sale alone lives your very attentive, faithful servant and compatriot who kisses your hands,

María del Pilar Sinués
April 12, 1892

*El Liberal,* April 13, 1892

*The Nineteenth Century: The Anarchist Teresa Claramunt*
*Describes Her Experiences in Jail*

### TERESA CLARAMUNT, 1862–1931

Claramunt was detained on suspicion of having participated in the 1896 Cambios Nuevos bombing in Barcelona. This excerpt is taken from notes solicited
and published by José Sempau, who wanted to publicize the suffering under-
gone by women and children at the hands of the government prosecuting
the crime. Claramunt dedicated her life as an anarchist to work on behalf of
workers, women, and children. In addition to organizing workers, she was a
publicist for the cause, writing plays and contributing to libertarian journals,
including La *Revista Blanca.*

### ⚮ *En la cárcel* ⚮

He padecido tanto, que no sé si podré coordinar mis recuerdos; pero
mi buen deseo seguramente me permitirá llenar este penoso cometido,
procurando que mi relación sea exacta y lo más concisa possible.

El dá 14 de Junio de 1896 tuve que abandonar la humilde casa en
que vivía con mi compañero Antonio Gurri. La guardia civil nos detuvo
en Camprodón y practicó en mis muebles un minucioso registro, que
más bien parecía un saqueo. Este acto produjo en nuestro ánimo una
impresión penosa y no pude contener mis lágrimas al ver que se nos
trataba como si fuéramos unos facinerosos, de los que no se podia es-
perar nada bueno.

Cuatro días después de mi detención y cuando se hubieron cansado
de marearme con preguntas irritantes, llevándome del juzgado al
goberno civil y de zeca en meca, me vi separada de mi compañero e
ingresé en la cárcel. En ésta me hallé con unas infelices mujeres detenidas como yo a consecuencia del crimen de Cambios Nuevos.

Los hierros candentes aplicados a los muslos del infortunado Nogués no le causaron quizá un dolor tan horrible como el que padecieron aquellas desgraciadas mujeres, que en su mayoría eran madres.

—¡Mis hijas en la calle sin pan ni albergue! exclamaba una de ellas, presa de la mayor desesperación. ¡Se perderán, se perderán y no volveré a verlas! Repetía llorando con desconsuelo.

—¡Las mías también! gritaba otra, derramando abundantes lágrimas. ¡Las llevarán al Hospicio y las matarán porque no saben rezar! ¡pobres hijitas, pobres pedazos de mi corazón!... Y sin poderlas ver... y seguía sollozando.

Todo esto lo presenció sor Juana, superiora de las hermanas de la cárcel; pero no se inmutó siquiera, demostrando la perversidad de sus sentimientos, que aun se evidencia mejor con lo que vamos a transcribir.

Y fue el caso que una de aquellas mujeres se dirigió a la superiora en tono de súplica, diciéndole:

—Por Dios, sor Juana, déjenos ver a nuestros pequeñuelos! ¡Somos inocentes!

—No puede ser, es imposible, respondió friamente la *hermana;* no son Vds. casadas, son malas y es menester que se vuelvan buenas...

Se nos trataba peor que a depravados criminales. Para nosotras no había cama, ni comunicación, ni enfermería, ni respeto, nada.

¡Cuánto sufrí moralmente durante los tres meses que estuve en la cárcel! ¡No puede concebirse! Mucho se ha hablado y con razón de los tormentos materiales, pero de los morales no hay nada escrito y sin embargo han causado muchas víctimas y ha dejado profunda huella en muchos organismos.

¡Cuánto sufrí y cuánto sufrieron mis compañeras durante nuestro cautiverio!

Un dia entró en calidad de presa una pobre vieja, más muerta que viva, y que lloraba amargamente. Nosotras las que estábamos detenidas como anarquistas fuimos a prestarle toda clase de consuelos, que bien las necesitaba. Calmada algún tanto, nos preguntó:

—¿Por qué están Vds. presas?

—Por un crimen que no hemos cometido. Por una bomba que la policía debe saber quién la echó.

—¡Qué! ¿son Vds. de las que suben a Montjuich? ¡Virgen santa! dijo con pena la anciana ¡si supiérais como les martirizan! Mi hija tiene relaciones con un militar que está en el castillo, y se halla ahora enfermo por haber presenciado los mártirios que se hacen con unos hombres que están a disposición de la guardia civil.

El efecto que nos produjo el anterior relato no es para descrito. Aquella noche tuve una horrible pesadilla. Mis compañeras me despertaron y noté que alguna lloraba.

Después oí la voz de la anciana que nos había comunicado lo que ocurría en Montjuich y que decía: ¡Pobres muchachos! ¡qué gritos daban de ¡asesinos! ¡soy inocente! No me atéis tan fuerte! ¡vosotros sois los autores!

Yo no me acordaba de nada, y noté que había llorado; el pecho me dolía, tenía fiebre.

## *In jail*

I have suffered so much that I do not know whether I shall be able to order my thoughts, but my sincere desire to do so will surely let me fulfill this painful task as I attempt to make my account as accurate and precise as possible.

On June 14, 1896, I had to leave the humble dwelling where I lived with my companion, Antonio Gurri. The Civil Guard detained us in Camprodón and went over my furniture so carefully that it seemed more like a sacking than a search. This action caused us considerable pain, and I could not keep from weeping when I saw that they were treating us as if we were criminals from whom nothing good could be expected.

Four days after my arrest and when they had tired of making me dizzy with irritating questions, taking me from court to the civil courthouse and from pillar to post, I found myself separated from my companion, and I was put in jail. There I encountered some wretched women who had been arrested, as I had been, in connection with the crime committed on Cambios Nuevos Street.

It is likely that the burning irons applied to the thighs of the unfortunate Nogués did not cause him as much pain as the pain those miserable women, most of whom were mothers, suffered.

One of them, in the grip of despair, exclaimed, "My daughters in the street without food or shelter!" Crying disconsolately, she repeated, "They will be lost, they will be lost, and I shall never see them again!"

Another woman, shedding abundant tears, cried, "Mine too! They will take them to the poorhouse, and they'll kill them there because they don't know how to pray! My poor little girls, poor little pieces of my heart! . . . And not to be able to see them . . ." And she kept on sobbing.

Sister Juana, mother superior of the sisters in the jail, saw all this, but she did not register anything, thereby showing how perverse she was, which becomes even clearer in view of what I am about to note.

This was that one of the women addressed her in a pleading tone, saying, "For the love of God, Sister Juana, let us see our little ones! We are innocent!"

The sister answered, "It cannot be; it is impossible. You are not married, you are evil, and it is necessary for you to reform . . ."

She treated us worse than if we had been depraved criminals. For us there were no beds, no communication with anyone outside, no infirmary privileges, no respect, nothing.

How I suffered morally during the three months I was in jail! It cannot be imagined! A lot has been said, and with reason, about physical torture, but nothing has been written about moral torture, and yet it left a profound imprint on the organisms of its many victims.

How much I suffered, and how much my companions suffered, during our imprisonment!

One day, an old woman, more dead than alive, entered the jail as a prisoner, weeping bitterly. Those of us who were detained there for being anarchists hastened to offer her the consolation she needed so badly. When she had calmed down a bit, she asked us, "Why have they put you in prison?"

"For a crime we have not committed. For throwing a bomb whose perpetrator the police surely know."

"What? Are you among the ones they are taking up to Montjuich? Holy Virgin!" the old woman cried. "If you knew how they are torturing people there! My daughter knows a military man who is in the castle, and he is sick now on account of having seen the torture the Civil Guard is applying to some men under their control."

The effect this piece of news had on us cannot be described. That night I had a horrible nightmare. My companions awakened me, and I saw that one of them was crying.

Later I heard the voice of the old woman who had told us about what was happening in Montjuich. She was saying, "Poor boys! How they cried out, 'Murderers! I am innocent! Don't tie me so tightly! You are the guilty ones!'"

I couldn't remember anything, and I realized that I had been crying; my chest hurt, and I had a fever.

Sempau 1900, 381–83

## Disasters of War in Cuba: A Witness to the Horror and Moral Corruption Brought About by Weyler's Reconcentration Policy

### MANUEL CIGES APARICIO, 1873–1936

Ciges was a Spanish journalist and novelist who enlisted for service in Cuba but soon found himself in opposition to General Weyler's policies, as well as to the war itself. As punishment for an article critical of Weyler's reconcentration policy that was to be published in the Parisian paper *L'Intransigeant,* Ciges was sentenced to more than four years in the dreaded La Cabaña prison in Havana. After his release, he wrote politically engaged fiction and dedicated himself to republican causes. Ciges was murdered by unidentified assassins in 1936. The following excerpt, taken from *Del cautiverio,* an account of the author's arrest and imprisonment from 1896 to 1898, contains the only reference I have found in the contemporary press, memoirs, letters, and literature to the sexual exploitation of minor females during the war. (Spanish women did not attain their majority until the age of twenty-five, but they were allowed to marry with parental permission by the age of twelve [Nelken 1975, 176, 172].)

Fue en Mariel donde visité la mansión de los reconcentrados. Al lado de una playa sucia, de aguas lívidas e inmóviles que exhalaban miasmas homicidas, alzábanse los sórdidos barracones de tostadas palmeras. Reinaba silencio de cementerio: ni una voz, ni un gemido. El mar dormía hipnotizado bajo los inmensos haces ígneos que el sol de mediodía le enviaba. De la tersa superficie opalina brotaban vivísimas refracciones, aúreo chisporroteo de hirviente metal que hería los ojos y aumentaba el cansancio del espíritu. Cuando llegué a este paraje de pesadilla y maldición, me detuve para escuchar. ¡Ni un rumor del mar, ni un suspiro de los hombres! Sólo barrunté en la cara el tácito pasar de un vaho caliginoso y repugnante. Era la muerte, callada e invisible soberana de la vasta necrópolis, que me azotaba desdeñosa el rostro.

Estaba perplejo. Si la curiosidad me inducía piadosa a conocer aquel moderno lugar de la expiación donde tantos seres fenecían diariamente, la prudencia me ordenaba alejarme presuroso. Indeciso y agobiado di la vuelta a los barracones, prestando atento oído; pero en todos prevalecía lúgubre silencio tumbal. Me detuve otra vez jadeante. Lo angustioso del paraje y el calor uniforme no entibiado por ningún hálito de la mar vecina, apenas me permitían respirar.

La compasión pudo más que el temor, y descorrí el andrajo que tapaba una puerta miserable.

¿Quién sino Dante, que visitó la region sombría donde sufren las sombras espectrales, podría describir este nuevo círculo del Infierno poblado de dolor y de patética repugnancia? Allí dentro, en aquel ambiente letal, vi revuelto montón de harapos y descarnados huesos: hombres, mujeres y niños; blancos y negros; vivos y muertos. Sobre desvencijado catre, sin colchón, ropa, ni cabezal, jadeaba un vestigio de mujer mal cubierto con los guiñapos de la mugrienta camisa que algunas horas después le serviría de sudario; porque la muerte tacituna habíala marcado ya con estigma imborrable en todo su ser: en el temblor convulso de los miembros, en la contracción de la boca purulenta. que no podia espantar una mosca impertinente que en ella se había posado, en la ancha franja cárdena que rodeaba las hondas cuencas donde se revolvían cansados los vidriosos ojos agonizantes. Abrazado a ella había un niño que, obstinándose en tomar leche, succionaba sangre en los flácidos pechos de su madre. Sentada en un cajón, a la vera del lecho, estaba la hija de la moribunda. Ni el hambre crónica ni la fiebre devastadora pudieron borrar de su carita macilenta los puros rasgos de criolla hermosura, realzada por sus enormes ojos negros de profundo y tristísimo mirar. Tenía el cuerpo encogido, enlazados bajo las agudas rodillas los finos dedos, amarillentos y exangües, para que al contacto de unos miembros con otros se prestase mutuo calor contra los frecuentes tamblores glaciales de la calentura. Tendido en el suelo dormitaba sudoroso y anhelante un anciano. A dos pasos de él acababa de expirar un negro. Al través de las rotas vestiduras, veíanse los huesos rígidos del africano en su inmovilidad de muerte. Ninguna mano piadosa le había cerrado los ojos, que ya no verían las iniquidades de los hombres, y en aquellas fijas pupilas no se leía nada: ni odio ni amor. Eran terribles, porque eran terriblemente indiferentes. Aun había otras personas en aquel tétrico tugurio: dos mujeres desgreñadas, revolviéndose trabajosamente dentro de sus viejas camisas y algunos chiquillos hambrientos y tristones, que me imploraban limosna extendiendo sus manos temblorosas de fiebre.

¡Qué sé yo de cuántas cosas me hablaron con acento débil y quejumbroso! Vecinos de la eternidad, todos esperaban confiados la muerte que les haría leve tan inacabable suplicio. Allí no había medicinas, pan, ni higiene. Nadie se acercaba a consolarles en su abandono irreparable. No era la resignación cristiana ni la sabiduría estoica, sino el lento acabamiento de las fuerzas vitales quien les había enseñado a no temer la muerte. La nada, el sumo descanso, era una necesidad para aquellos seres borrados ya de entre los vivos... ¡Todos estaban condenados a perecer en breve plazo. Secadas sus existencias por la fiebre amarilla!...

También sentía yo fiebre. Denso sudor helado me inundaba la frente, y en la garganta barruntaba contracciones de mortal angustia. Me acerqué a la puerta para respirar. ¡Con qué avidez contemplé el cielo azul y el mar extenso, que seguía en imperturbable calma de plácido dormer! ¿Habría más allá de aquel remoto horizonte circular, donde cielo y mar se confundían, una patria más piadosa para tanta víctima como allí dentro gemía olvidada de los hombres?

La hija de la moribunda se acercó penosamente a la puerta, y tras larga dubitación me pidió algunas monedas para comer. Ella me ofrecía, en cambio, un amor imposible de aceptar.

Luego supe que la concupiscencia soldadesca iba frecuentemente a profanar aquella carne que olía a sepulcro.

Sólo tuve valor de recorrer tres departamentos, y en todos vi igual repugnante abandono. Al retirarme tenía la convicción de que dejaba doscientos condenados a muerte, que se renovarían mientras durase la guerra.

........................

It was in Mariel that I visited the quarters of the *reconcentrados*. Miserable barracks constructed of dark palm fronds stood next to a dirty beach whose grayish, stagnant standing water exuded a deadly miasma. It was as silent as a cemetery: not a voice or a groan to be heard. The sea slept hypnotized beneath the sky, its surface pierced by the immense fiery shafts that the midday sun cast into it. Lively reflections sprang from its smooth, opalescent surface, a golden burst of burning metallic sparks that hurt your eyes and drained your spirit. When I reached this cursed and nightmarish place, I stopped to listen. Not a single sound from the sea, not one sigh from a human voice! I sensed only a warm, disgusting vapor passing silently by my face. It was death, the quiet and invisible sovereign of the vast necropolis, that was disdainfully brushing past me.

I did not know what to do. If pious curiosity led me to examine that modern site of expiation where so many human beings were dying every day, prudence urged me to withdraw from it quickly. Undecided and exhausted, I walked around the barracks, listening carefully. But a sepulchral silence reigned in every one of them. Gasping for air, I stopped again. The desolate site was making me anxious, and the heat, unrelieved by any movement of air from the nearby sea, scarcely allowed me to breathe.

Compassion prevailed over fear, and I pushed aside the bit of rag draped over a wretched door.

Except for Dante, who visited the gloomy region where spectral shades suffer eternally, who could describe this new circle of Hell, this pathetically repulsive abode of pain? Inside the hut, in the still, lethal air, I saw a jumble of rags, skin, and bones: men and women and children; whites and blacks; the living and the dead. What was left of a woman lay fighting for breath on a bare, broken-down cot without bedclothes or headrest. Her only covers were the tatters of a soiled blouse that would serve her later as a shroud, for silent death had marked her whole being with its ineffaceable stigmata, visible in the convulsive trembling of her limbs, in the contractions of her pus-covered mouth, too weak to dislodge a nagging fly that had alighted there, in the wide red rims that bordered the deep sockets in which her weary, dying, glassy eyes rolled helplessly. Clinging to her was a child who, obstinately persistent in getting milk, was sucking blood from her flaccid breasts. The dying woman's daughter was seated on a box at the edge of the bed. Neither chronic hunger nor a devastating fever could efface the traces of an authentic Creole beauty from her thin face, beauty enhanced by her enormous black eyes with their profoundly sad gaze. She was bent forward, her thin, yellowish, waxen fingers interlaced under her sharp knees so that the contact of one part of her body with another might lend mutual warmth against the recurrent, icy chills brought on by fever. An old man lay stretched out on the floor. A black man had just died a few feet away from him. Through his torn clothing you could see the African's bones rigid in the immobility of death. No pious hand had closed his eyes, which would no longer look upon the iniquity of men, and you couldn't read anything in those fixed pupils, neither love nor hate. They were terrible because they were terribly indifferent. There were other people in that gloomy hole: two disheveled women in ragged blouses turning over and over with great difficulty and some hungry, wretched children, who held out hands shaking with fever to beg me for alms.

How can I convey what they said to me in weak, querulous voices? Near neighbors of eternity, they all confidently awaited the death that would relieve their unending torture. There was no medicine, food, or provision made for hygiene in that place. No one came to console them in their irreparable abandonment. It was not Christian resignation or stoical wisdom, but rather the slow decline of vital forces, that taught them not to fear death. Nothingness, total rest was now a necessity for those creatures already erased from among the living . . . They were all condemned to perish in a short while, their lives extinguished by yellow fever . . . !

I also felt feverish. A cold, copious sweat covered my forehead, and I felt a tightening in my throat caused by a deadly sense of anguish. I went to the door to get a breath of air. How anxiously I contemplated the blue sky and the wide sea, which remained imperturbably calm in its placid slumber. Beyond the distant, round horizon where sky and sea meet, would there be a more compassionate homeland for the many victims who were groaning inside this place forgotten by mankind?

The dying woman's daughter approached the door and after a long pause asked me for a few coins for food. She offered me in exchange an act of love I could not accept.

Later I learned that lust frequently led soldiers to that place in order to profane the flesh that already smelled of the grave.

I only had the heart to look at three more huts, and in each one I saw the same repugnant abandonment. When I left, I was convinced that I was leaving two hundred people condemned to death, a number that would be renewed for as long as the war lasted.

Ciges Aparicio 1930, 2–4

*The Nineteenth Century: The Cost of Conscription; The End of the Cuban and Philippine Insurrections*

ÁNGELES LÓPEZ DE AYALA, 1856–1910

Journalist, novelist, and playwright, Ángeles López de Ayala was a feminist, the founder of a lay organization similar to the Red Cross, El Nivel Rojo, a freethinker and founder of journals (*El Progreso* and *El Libertador*) that promulgated libertarian ideas. She was imprisoned three times for her beliefs. The following article appeared nine days after the United States sank the Spanish fleet under the command of Admiral Cervera in Santiago Bay and one month before Spain recognized the loss of Cuba and Puerto Rico, on August 12, 1898.

¡¡Doscientos mil hombres!!

De este número se compondrá el ejército de la Península.

Doscientos mil hombres formarán en las filas militares, aumentando con dicho contingente las cargas del Estado.

En cambio, las familias se disminuirán, pero cabalmente por el individuo que, en general, las mantenía; por el mancebo robusto, honrado y trabajador, que a cambio de su sudor les proporcionaba el pan, y que ahora irá a contra pasos y a sufrir las genialidades de los que se llaman sus superiores, abdicando de su libre albedrío, de su criterio y de su voluntad.

Quedan, pues en el mayor desamparo, los ancianos, las mujeres y los niños.

Pero, ¡no importa!

Para los ancianos que disponen de alguna *influencia*, están las casas de caridad, y para los que ninguna tienen, ahí están las *cocinas económicas*, lugar de ensayo para que en él se amaestren en la repartición de la *sopa conventual*, los que sin duda ocuparán el puesto de *donados*, en las nuevas y numerosas comunidades religiosas masculinas, que en breve llegarán de lo que ya no sera colonia española, y en donde por tanto, no podrá albergarse la holganza y el estacionamiento.

Por lo que toca a las mujeres, como se trata de humildes hijas del pueblo, la opinión no ha de ocuparse de este asunto; que vayan a trabajar en las pocas fábricas que no se cierran, o que se hagan simpáticas al fabricante o al mayordomo; o, si son viejas, que aprendan a no comer; porque, en el ultimo caso, el gobierno no tiene la culpa de que ellas no hayan nacido duquesas.

Y respecto a los niños... esto ya ofrece una solución más fácil.

¿Que no la adivináis, lectores nuestros?

Pues es sin duda, porque no habréis ido nunca a los muelles de nuestras poblaciones marítimas; pues de lo contrario, en ellos hubiérais visto un ejército, más numeroso aún que el que el señor Correa otorga a la Península, y que a semejanza de éste vive a expensas del país, con la diferencia de que asienta sus *cuarteles* al aire libre, y que sus ejercicios se llaman *raterías*.

Ya veis, pues, cómo el problema de los niños abandonados está resuelto, y cómo nuestro ministro de la Guerra, hace *perfectamente* en disponer de la gente útil para el trabajo (que además no se encontrará) y cuán misericordiosa es la sociedad presente, ya que hasta por medio de sus vicios, proporciona sustento a los necesitados.

¿Pero, qué hemos dicho? ¿Los vicios de la sociedad? ¿Por ventura, la sociedad los tiene?

Está en el uso de la palabra los reyes, los príncipes, los magnates los frailes, las monjas el clero, los sacristanes, y hasta los monaguillos...

Por nuestra parte, hemos de decir que no debe tenerlos, porque hemos quedado, según nuestros restauradores, en que vivimos en el major de los mundos, y en que, por consiguiente, cualquier reforma resulta extemporánea.

Es decir: a excepción de las trascendentales reformas que nuestros inteligentes ministros introduzcan en sus respectivos ramos.

Y con especialidad, nuestro immortal ministro de Marina.

¡Nada, nada! Declaramos lisa y llanamente que somos partidarios de los 200,000 soldados para la Península, y que felicitamos al Sr. Correa por su disposición, que nos resarcirá (es un decir) de la pérdida de nuestras colonias, y que nos librará de que los Yankees bombardeen nuestros puertos, como impidió la escuadra de Cervera el golpe destructor con que la había amenazado.

Y que vayan chillando los enemigos de lo existente. Que en el caso de convenir, ya se les hará chillar con los fusiles de los consabidos 200,000 hombres.

¡Pues no faltaba más, si no que las instituciones quedaran a merced del populacho! ¡Eso sería bueno si se tratara de un regimen que con el *populacho* simpatizara!

Pero vayan ustedes a buscar las simpatías de nuestro regimen en la masa anónima del país.

O en las colonias.

O entre las madres pobres...

En resumen: que Correa tiene razón, y que los espanoles también la tendremos para sufrir resignados nuestras penas cuando el ministro vea logrado su propósito y 200,000 madres se hayan quedado sin sus hijos.

Y... ¡Viva Espana!

Y... ¡Viva la restauración!

Y... ¡¡¡Correa con sus 200,000 hombres!!!

Ángeles López de Ayala

Día de gracia, 12 de julio de 1898

...................

Two hundred thousand men!!

This is the number of men who will compose the Peninsular army.

Two hundred thousand men will fill the military ranks, said contingent thereby increasing the charges of the State.

In exchange, families will become smaller precisely on account of the individual who in general maintained them; on account of the robust, honorable, and hardworking youth who with his sweat provided them with bread and who will now go off to march in step and to suffer the brilliant ideas of those who call themselves his superiors, abdicating his free will, his judgment, and his volition.

There remain, then, in the worst state of helplessness, old people, women, and children.

But it doesn't matter!

There are charity houses for old people who wield some *influence,* and for those who have none there are the *economy kitchens,* a place to rehearse and train in how to distribute *convent soup,* a job useful to those who will occupy the place of assistants in the new and numerous male religious communities that will shortly arrive from what will no longer be a Spanish colony and where, therefore, neither laziness nor slackness will find a home.

As for women, since we are dealing with humble daughters of the people, public opinion need not concern itself with this matter. Let them go to work in the few factories that do not close, or let them make themselves agreeable to the factory owner or the foreman; or if they are old, let them learn how not to eat, because in the final analysis, the government is not to blame for their not having been born duchesses.

And with respect to the children . . . this presents a simpler solution.

You can't guess what it is, faithful readers?

Well, doubtless that is because you have never ventured down to the wharves of our maritime cities, since if you had, you would have seen there an army that is even more numerous than the one Sr. Correa is granting to the Peninsula and that like it lives at the expense of the country, with the difference that the former has its *barracks* in the open air and its exercises are called *petty thievery*.

You see then how the problem of abandoned children is resolved, and how our Minister of War acts perfectly well in disposing of people useful for work (which in fact will not be found), and you see, also, how charitable our present society is, since even its vices contribute to the maintenance of those in need.

But what have we said? The vices of society? Is it possible that society harbors vices?

The word is used by kings, princes, magnates, friars, nuns, the clergy, sacristans, and even altar boys . . .

As for us, we are compelled to say that society cannot possibly harbor vices, because we have all acknowledged, according to our restorers, that we live in the best of all worlds and therefore any reform would be inopportune.

That is, with the exception of the transcendental reforms that our intelligent ministers introduce in their respective branches of government.

And most especially our immortal Minister of the Navy.

Well and good! Well and good! We declare purely and simply that we are in favor of the 200,000 soldiers for the Peninsula and that we congratulate Sr. Correa for his administrative order, which will compensate us (in a manner of speaking) for the loss of our colonies and which will prevent the Yankees from bombarding our ports, just as Cervera's squadron warded off the destructive blow with which it was threatened.

And let the enemies of what exists go about screaming if they wish. And if it seems appropriate, the rifles of the ubiquitous 200,000 men will make them scream even more.

Well, that would be the limit—institutions at the mercy of the mob! Wouldn't it be splendid if it were a question of a government that sympathized with the *mob!*

Go look for any sympathy on the part of our regime for the anonymous mass of the country.

Or for the colonies.

Or for poor mothers . . .

In sum, Correa is right, and we Spaniards will also be right to suffer our sorrows with resignation when the minister shall have achieved his goal and 200,000 mothers have been left without their sons.

And . . . Long live Spain!

And . . . Long live the Restoration!

And . . . Correa with his 200,000 men!!!

Ángeles López de Ayala

Day of grace, July 12, 1898

La Conciencia Libre (Valencia), July 14, 1898

## The End of the Century: A Female Freethinker Earns the Respect of Male Colleagues

### SOLEDAD GUSTAVO (TERESA MAÑÉ I MIRAVET), 1865–1939

Soledad Gustavo was introduced to anarchist thought as a young girl and remained dedicated to libertarian ideals throughout her life. She worked as a teacher in a school that promoted free thought before marrying Juan Montseny (pseudonym, Federico Urales), with whom she edited La Revista Blanca and Tierra y Libertad. Their daughter, Federica Montseny, was a prominent libertarian figure in Spain before and during the Second Republic. By 1903 Tierra y Libertad had become the mouthpiece for anarchism in Spain. Gustavo continued to write and work during the Civil War and died in Perpignan a few days after crossing the border into exile.

The article extracted below describes a meeting attended by anarchists, federalists, socialists, unitary republicans, and unaffiliated liberals that was held in the Centro Federal in Madrid in late September 1899 to honor all deceased freethinkers. Four men and one woman, Soledad Gustavo, took part in the formal presentation. The meeting began with a denunciation of Catholics and Carlists for placing plaques depicting the Sacred Heart of Jesus in various cities and towns throughout Spain. The organizers of the meeting also condemned the opposition of the governor of Madrid to the Society of Locksmiths' wish to grant funds to secular schools. Sr. Corona then delivered a comparative study

of religions in which he concluded that all religions were pernicious. He attributed the rise in religious "spirit" to the repressive law against anarchism (July
1896), urged greater propaganda efforts on the part of anarchists, and recalled
deceased freethinkers, including Miguel Servet, "iniquitously immolated by the
enemies of science." Sr. Navarro then spoke about free thought in the empire
of Morocco, affirming that there were more freethinkers there than in Spain.

---

Doña Soledad Gustavo, que al levantarse a hablar fue saludada con una general salva de aplausos, leyó con notable corrección un extenso y hermoso
trabajo, en el que convencida de que defendiendo sus ideas honraba
mejor la memoria de los librepensadores fallecidos, expuso muy clara y
extensamente sus opiniones sobre el origin y las causas de los males sociales, afirmando, entre otros conceptos, que aquellas causas son prin-
cipalmente: Dios y el capital. Esperamos leerlo detenidamente, porque
suponemos que verá la luz pública, un discurso tan notable como el
de Dona Soledad Gustavo, la infatigable propagandista y radical pensadora.

El Sr. Castells, en nombre de la Sociedad, dio las gracias por su concurso al público, a los oradores y muy especialmente a Doña Soledad
Gustavo, que al tomar parte en la velada había demostrado dos cosas:
la inteligencia y las condiciones de carácter de la mujer, condiciones
que la igualan al hombre. Con este motivo se extendió el Sr. Castells
a demostrar la injusticia cometida por la sociedad actual con el mal
llamado sexo débil, y encareció la necesidad de defender la instrucción
y la dignificación de la mujer.

Dirigió un saludo a todos los librepensadores del mundo, especialmente a los de Roma que conmemoraban el día siguiente el aniversario
de su entrada en la corte del Papa, hecho que constituyó su mayor victoria contra la reacción.

Hizo una reseña de las principales luchas religiosas que la humanidad ha tenido, consignando el fabuloso número de víctimas a que han
dado lugar. Afirmó que la última guerra sostenida con los tagalos había
sido ocasionada por la intolerancia religiosa. Llamó la atención sobre el
incremento que toman los reaccionarios en la vieja Europa, incremento
demostrado por la reciente condena de Dreyfus, y la existencia en pie

de la odiosa Bastilla catalana llamada Montjuich. Dedicó frases de admiración a la República del Ecuador, que en pocos años ha pasado de católica y levítica a partidaria de la libertad de cultos.

Dijo que en España era actualmente tal el movimiento de los reaccionarios que había necesidad de aprestarse a una lucha decidida con ellos si se quería salvar lo más esencial de las libertades. Expuso en prueba de sus afirmaciones los sucesos de Castellón, Vinaroz, Salamanca, Tolosa y otros puntos con motivo de la colocación de las placas del corazón de Jesús; el desenfado e impunidad con que hacen su propaganda de acción los carlistas, como se ha visto en Burriana; el cáracter marcadamente reaccionario de los últimos gobiernos liberales y conservadores, los primeros de los cuales impusieron la obligación de estudiar religión en la segunda enseñanza, reforma ampliada notablemente por el gobierno actual, cuyo plan de enseñanza obliga a estudiar cuatro años de religion y seis de latín; el inconcebible propósito de los congresistas de Burgos de constituir un partido politico llamado católico, en cuyo programa figura la supresión del laicismo en la enseñanza, el restablecimiento de la censura y del fuero eclesiástico, la ley del descanso dominical, la clausura de todas las sociedades que no sean católicas, la libertad académica de la Iglesia; la exención del servicio militar de los seminaristas y otra porción de ventajas para la Iglesia, tan enormemente absurdas como esas.

"Si no nos aprestamos a defendernos," dijo, "pronto veremos funcionar a los sicarios del Santo Oficio, practicando el auto de fe y las espantosas crueldades con que se hicieron célebres en los pasados tiempos.

Es preciso que nos unamos como aquí se ha dicho; pero para unirnos no precisa que celebremos pactos ni contratos previos que sólo conducen a la confusión y a la pérdida de energías en las colectividades que los llevan a cabo. Sólo hace falta, que al igual que hemos venido todos a esta velada, en la que hay anarquistas, federales, socialistas, republicanos unitarios y liberales no políticos, acudamos todos también para defenderla a donde quiera que peligre la libertad de conciencia.

Al programa de la reacción debemos nosotros oponer el nuestro amplio, definido, hermoso, imitando en nuestra propaganda a los queridos correligionarios nuestros Arús, Gálvez Arce, Bartrina, Fletcher, Martínez Conde, Brunette y de más [sic] que aquí se ha nombrado esta noche.

Esta propaganda debe ser activa y sostenida, y cuando llegue el momento, que llegará, de la lucha por la fuerza, cuando la revolución, cualquiera que sea su origin, sea un hecho, es preciso que los librepensadores no olvidemos que nuestra más importante misión es barrer para siempre hasta el recuerdo de la superstición religiosa, en la seguridad de que haremos un gran bien a la humanidad, y de que por muy sangrienta que sea nuestra acción, sera un leve desahogo comparada con las monstruosas hecatombes producidas [en] el mundo por los reaccionarios."

Todos los oradores fueron muy aplaudidos por la numerosa concurrencia que llenaba completamente el local.

........................

Doña Soledad Gustavo, who was greeted with a general salvo of applause when she rose to speak, read most ably an extensive and beautiful paper in which, convinced that she was honoring the memory of deceased freethinkers by defending her ideas on the subject, she proceeded to expound clearly and at length her ideas on the origin and causes of social ills, affirming, among other ideas, that there are two principal causes for those ills: God and capitalism. When it becomes available to the public, as we suppose it will, we hope to read at our leisure this notable study by Doña Soledad Gustavo, the indefatigable propagandist and radical thinker.

Sr. Castells, in the name of the Society, thanked the public for attending and the speakers for their presentations, with special thanks to Doña Soledad Gustavo, who, in taking part in the meeting, had demonstrated two things: the intelligence and the resources of character found in women, conditions that make them equal to men. In this connection Sr. Castells pointed out the injustice committed by society with respect to the wrongly denominated weaker sex, emphasizing the need to defend education and contribute to the dignifying of women.

Sr. Castells saluted all the freethinkers in the world, and especially those in Rome, who would commemorate the following day their entry into the Papal court, an event that constituted a major victory against reaction.

He reviewed the principal religious battles humanity had suffered and the huge number of victims they had caused. He affirmed that the recent war against the Tagalos had been caused by religious intolerance and called attention to the increase in religious reaction sweeping old Europe, an increase evidenced by the Dreyfus affair and the existence of the odious Catalan Bastille called Montjuich. He praised the Republic of Ecuador, which within a few years had evolved from a Catholic, priest-ridden state to one that recognized freedom of religion.

He said that the reactionary movement in Spain was such that it was necessary to mount a decided campaign against it if the most basic liberties were to be salvaged. In proof of his assertions he mentioned the events in Castellón, Vinaroz, Salamanca, Tolosa, and other places that had occurred as a result of placing plaques depicting the sacred heart of Jesus; the self-confidence and impunity with which the Carlists carry on their propaganda by acts, as was seen in Burriana; the markedly reactionary character of recent liberal and conservative governments, the first of which imposed the study of religion in secondary schools, a directive notably broadened by the current government, whose plan mandates four years of religion and six of Latin; the unthinkable proposal of the representatives from Burgos to form a political party denominated Catholic, whose program would call for the suppression of secularism in education, the reestablishment of censorship and ecclesiastical law, the law of Sunday rest, the closing of all societies that are not Catholic, the academic freedom of the Church, the exemption of seminarians from military duty, and other advantages for the Church as incredibly absurd as these.

"If we do not hasten to defend ourselves," he said, "we will soon see the assassins of the Holy Office conducting autos da fe along with other infamous acts of cruelty notorious in times past.

"It is necessary that we unite, as has been said here; but in order to unite it is not necessary to celebrate pacts or contracts, which only lead to confusion and the loss of energy in the collectivities that bring them about. All that is needed is that we come together, just as we have all—anarchists, federalists, socialists, unitary republicans, and nonaligned liberals—come together in this meeting, to defend freedom of conscience.

"We must oppose our broad, well-defined, beautiful program to the program of reaction by imitating through our propaganda our beloved coreligionists, Arús, Gálvez Arce, Bartrina, Fletcher, Martínez Conde, Brunette, and others whom we have named here tonight.

"This propaganda must be active and sustained, and when the moment comes for the outbreak of the struggle by force, when the revolution, whatever its origin, becomes a reality, it is important that we freethinkers do not forget that our most important mission is to sweep away forever even the memory of religious superstition, in the secure belief that we will perform a great service for humanity and that however bloody our actions may be, they will constitute a minor discomfort compared with the monstrous hecatombs produced by reactionaries."

All the speakers received great applause from the numerous public that completely filled the hall.

*El Nuevo Régimen,* September 23, 1899, 3

## The Turn of the Century: Women and Mothers Must Cast Off Traditional Habits of Mind and Action

### TERESA CLARAMUNT, 1862–1931

The excerpt that follows is taken from Claramunt's essay *Women: General Considerations on Their Condition in Light of Men's Prerogatives*, published in 1905 and distributed gratis.

Esta ausencia de sentimientos y costumbres sanas [en el hogar español] nos lleva a tomar en serio una infinidad de disparates que se observan en otros órdenes de la vida, y que serían objeto de chacota si más tarde no resultaran un suplicio para nuestros hijos. ¿Quién no ha visto a una mujer hacer alardes de sus sentimientos maternales, llorar a lágrima viva al notar que su hijo está enfermo, disputar con las vecinas porque le han reñido y separarlo del corro de los grandotes para que no oiga frases que juzga reñidas con la moral? Pues, en cambio, esa misma madre pronuncia en presencia del mismo hijo mil perrerías, a cual más grosera, por cualquier cuestión que haya tenido con las vecinas, o le refiere con tono beatífico todo un tejido de patrañas y embustes místico-religiosos o le mete en cualquier escuela, sin importarle que el profesor sea un jesuita, una fiera ordenancista.

Todos los días conmueve nuestros nervios el rugido que contra el despotismo levanta la protesta popular, y, a pesar de todo, no reparamos en adorar el símbolo de este despotismo, regalando a los niños, en determinadas festividades, juguetes que representan espadas, fusiles, soldados, y también nos permitimos la alegría de verles seguir mascaradas del carnaval luciendo los entorchados del bárbaro conquistador o la casaca enconchada del parásito privilegiado.

La tarea que me he impuesto requiere muchas observaciones para dejar afirmado que el celo de las madres en favor de sus hijos está luego negado por los hechos, y que el afán de que se alardea por sacudir la dominación del tirano resulta vago, inconsciente, desde el momento que en los más sencillos actos de la vida aparece el fantasma de la tradición, obstáculo tenaz a toda positiva manifestación sana.

❈

Vamos a concretar.

Todos los privilegios causa del desequilibrio social existente, todas las guerras que con tanta frecuencia desolan a la humanidad, todo el conjunto de dolores y atrocidades que tan de cerca nos hieren y conmuevan, hallan apoyo en la ignorancia de esa media humanidad que constituyen las mujeres, ignorancia que perpetúa, con los prejuicios señalados, la otra mitad, compuesta por los hombres.

Examinen estos su obra, examínenla y verán cómo sus orgullos, sus prerrogativas, sus códigos, sus religiones, forman la roca que les aplasta. Su extrema fatiga no hallará descanso hasta que no borren las limitaciones que impusieron a la mujer por temor de que no derrumbase el hogar de sus egoismos. [...]

Es menester también que la mujer no espere únicamente del hombre el remedio a sus males. Ella misma debe emplear todo el esfuerzo propio para levantarse de la postración en que ha vivido. No quiera ver encadenadas por más tiempo sus acciones.

Obrando así, con consciencia propia de sus derechos y de sus deberes, el concurso que el hombre le preste contribuirá eficazmente a completar la transformación imperiosamante necesaria.

........................

This lack of genuine sentiment and wholesome conduct [in the typical Spanish home] leads us to take seriously an endless number of absurdities observable in other aspects of family life that would be a source of amusement if they did not turn into a later cause of suffering for our sons. Who has not seen a woman displaying her maternal sentiments, crying her eyes out when her son was sick, entering into a dispute with the neighbors because they had scolded him, and separating him from the bigger boys so that he wouldn't hear things that she considered improper? Then that same mother turns around and, in the presence of her son, uses language that gets increasingly ugly and gross because of some disagreement with the neighbors. Or, in a beatific tone, she regales him with a tissue of mystical-religious prettified lies and tall tales. Or she puts him in just any school without bothering to find out whether the teacher is a Jesuit, a rigid and cruel taskmaster.

Every day the roar of popular protest against despotism jangles our nerves, yet in spite of it all we do not hesitate to pay homage to the symbol of this despotism by giving our sons gifts such as swords, rifles, and toy soldiers on festive occasions, and we permit ourselves the joy of watching them follow after carnival maskers displaying the braided insignia of the barbarous conquistador or the shell-like cassock of the privileged parasite.

My self-imposed task requires that I provide many examples in order to demonstrate that the zeal of mothers is later negated by their actions and that their boastful desire to throw off the domination of the tyrant turns out to be vague and unmindful from the moment when the phantasm of tradition, the tenacious obstacle to all healthy positive action, makes its appearance and proceeds to govern the simplest acts in life.

※||※

Let us be specific.

All the privileges that constitute the cause of our current social disequilibrium, all the wars that so often devastate humanity, all the sorrows and atrocities that wound us and move us so intimately owe their support to the ignorance of the half of humanity composed of women, an ignorance that the other half, composed of men, perpetuates, guided by all the prejudices pointed out above.

Let men examine their work; let them examine it, and they will see how their pride, their prerogatives, their legal codes, and their religions have formed the boulder that is crushing them. The extreme fatigue produced by this heavy burden will never be relieved until they erase the limitations that they have imposed on women out of fear that the structure of home and hearth produced by their egoisms would collapse. [. . .]

Women must not expect the remedy for all their ills to come exclusively from men. Women themselves must employ all their strength to lift themselves up from the state of prostration in which they have been living. Let them never again find their capacity to act hindered by the chains that have bound them up to now.

If they work in this way, with full consciousness of their rights and duties, the help that men will give women will contribute effectively to complete the transformation that is so urgently needed.

Claramunt 1905, 16–19

# Notes

## Introduction

*Epigraph:* Emilio Castelar, from his commentary on a painting, *Viernes Santo,* reproduced in *La Ilustración Artística* (Barcelona), April 15, 1889, 133. "[Se ven las] penas de María en las cimas del Calvario, donde atraviesan su corazón todos los horrores que puede una madre sentir aquí en la vida. Para comprenderlos necesitamos tan sólo recordar el claro ministerio cedido por la naturaleza y por la Providencia de consuno a la madre. Sólo un amor como el suyo podría superar los dolores conjuntos a la gestación, al parto, a la crianza de sus hijos. Por eso en la maternidad ha puesto Dios invencibles propensiones al sacrificio que parecen como un suicidio lento y que son un holocausto perpetuo."

1. For the total amount of commutation fees collected by the government, see Hernández Sandoica and Mancebo 1978, 370. For a concise account of conscription in Spain from 1868 to 1912, see Puell de la Villa 1996, 272–301. There is an excellent overview of conscription in the nineteenth century in Sales de Bohigas 1968. For a clear exposition of the social and economic implications of the system of commutation in place in Spain from 1850 to 1912, see Sales de Bohigas 1974, 215–17. The law of *reclutamiento y reemplazo del ejército* was published in the November 1896 issue of the *Boletín de Legislación y Jurisprudencia.* An annotated edition with commentary was published by the *Revista de Tribunales* in the same year.

2. See Fernández Almagro 1969, 379; Serrano 1984, 86–87, 98–99; and Balfour 1997, 95–96.

3. My thanks to John T. O'Connor for pointing out the connection between the *levée en masse* and Castelar's exhortation, which may be found in Castelar 1874, 153–54. Castelar was fond of this formulation and repeated it often in his moral admonitions to the Spanish people.

## 1. Spanish Women and War, 1808–1898

*Epigraph:* Pérez Galdós 1950, 1245. "Sí, al mismo tiempo que expiraba la gran lucha internacional, daba sus primeros vagidos la Guerra Civil; del majestuoso seno ensangrentado y destrozado de la una salió la otra, cual si de él naciera. Como Hércules, empezó a hacer atrocidades desde la cuna."

1. According to Micheal Clodfelter, the casualties in the Carlist Wars, not counting civilians, numbered 140,000 during the first war (1832–40), 10,000 in the second

(1846–49), and 50,000 in the third (1872–76). Clodfelter 2001, 197–98. For the combined Confederate and Union soldiers killed in action in the Civil War, see ibid., 331–32. The statistics noted here, which do not include civilian deaths, do not represent the truly staggering toll on the lives of the inhabitants of Spain or the United States, where total Civil War deaths numbered more than 700,000. See also Oyarzun 1969; Holt 1967; Clemente 1982; and Canal 2000.

2. See Cambronero 1891.

3. For an article written during the second Cuban insurrection recalling women's role in the War of Independence and expressing the above view, see Zamora y Caballero 1895. For a modern account, see Tone 1999. Tone's concern is to discover how women resisted the enemy, whether their actions transgressed gender boundaries, and why their participation in the war effort did not change their status in Spanish society.

4. Erauso 1829. See also Erauso 1992; Merrim 1999; and Velasco 2000.

5. See Gómez de Arteche 1875, xix.

6. Rafael Monje published a brief account of the life of the Varona de Villanañe in the *Semanario Pintoresco Español* (Madrid) in 1848. This and the following information concerning La Varona is taken from the Hijos de J. Espesa 1929, 92–93.

7. Canel refers to herself as the Monja Alférez in her *Albúm de la trocha* (1897). For Catalina de Erauso's life and honors, see Merrim 1999, chap. 1. Many women warriors figure in Spain's past. For a long list of female fighters, with a commentary on each one, see Burgos 1927, 231–47. I have narrowed my focus to those women whose feats drew comment in the press and literature of the 1870s to 1890s. For an exploration of the parallels between the two women, see Walker 2006.

8. "La mujer ha sido siempre el sostén, el aliento y hasta la compañera del soldado en nuestra tierra. Con su espíritu le ha animado en todas las contiendas, y si nuestras guerras civiles han sido tan reñidísimas, ha sido por la parte que en ellas han tomado las mujeres. Durante la guerra de la Independencia no hubo madre que, aunque se le desgarrase el corazón, quisiera detener a su hijo en el hogar, y todas los alentaba a pelear por la patria. Cuando en el sitio de Zaragoza faltaron hombres para disparar los cañones, los dispararon las mujeres, y no se olvidará nunca, cuando de hazañas heroicas se trate, ni a Agustina Aragón ni a la condesa de Bureta.

La mujer, débil y tímida en los trances ordinarios de la vida, se transforma en los momentos supremos y lleva a cabo las más grandes heroicidades." *La Ilustración Ibérica* (Madrid), August 31, 1895, 546. See the appendix for an appreciation of the actions taken by the Countess of Bureta during the War of Independence.

9. Kate Masterson's interview with General Weyler was published in Green 1896, in the chapter "How Women Fight in Cuba." I have seen a reference to a book by Enrique Ubieta, *La mujer en la revolución cubana* (Havana, ca. 1911), which may contain information on women combatants, but I have not been able to locate a copy. Teresa Prados-Torreira informs me that Ubieta published an article entitled "La mujer cubana en la revolución" in *Bohemia*, December 24, 1910, 394, and may have printed this or another article as

a small book later, which was common practice at the time. Chapter 1 of Stoner 1991 has material on women fighters. There is a reference to *mambisas* (female rebels) who fought alongside men in Ferrer 1998, 679. See also Nuez González 1978; Álvarez Estévez 1976; and Prados-Torreira 2005. Soriano 1995b provides an up-to-date account of the women who actually participated in combat in the Philippines. During the Philippine insurrection and the American invasion that followed, women nursed the wounded, the sick, and the orphaned. They also established and organized local and national chapters of the Red Cross. For more information on this aspect of their participation, see Tiongson 2004, 197.

10. In an article published in *El País* on March 7, 2005, noting the bicentennial exposition and publications dedicated to Juana de la Vega (1805–72), the wife of General Espoz y Mina, Amelia Castilla writes that Juana "even went so far as to take part in the war [the first Carlist conflict], and the soldiers referred to her as 'the lady general'" (llegó, incluso, a participar en la guerra y los soldados la llamaban "la generala"). I have found no confirmation of this assertion either in Vega Martínez 1977 or elsewhere.

11. "Cierto; la Guerra es una infracción de la ley de Dios, un escarnio de sus mandamientos, un atentado contra todos los derechos, un olvido de todos los deberes: ella honra lo que es infame, patrocina lo que es vil, y no hay impiedad que no sancione ni protervia que no justifique." Arenal 1942, 92.

12. Benito Pérez Galdós created a similar character in María Egipciaca, of *La familia de León Roch* (1879). Similar in the sense that each woman's repressed sexuality found expression in acts and aspirations harmful to a *bien-pensant*, bourgeois society.

13. Feijóo Gómez 1996, 444–45.

No griten libertad los españoles
No digan que en España la tenemos
Que en bandera de más honores lleva
Cada soldado amarra una cadena,
Y cada madre llora en sus hogares
La pérdida del hijo más querido
Y en el llanto que vierte su agonía
Maldice de la ley la tiranía.
No hay libertad donde la madre llora
Y al ver crecer su hijo, deseara
Que la mano del cielo lo lisiara.
¿Quién es la ley para marcar de esclavo
Al joven que cumplió los veinte abriles?
Quien toque un ser que libre un padre cría
No se llama Ley, sí tiranía.

14. Ibid., 445.

15. Ramón y Cajal 1939, 253. During the anticlerical violence in Barcelona in 1909 the asylum on Calle Aldana run by the Sisters of Charity felt the wrath of workers who

believed that the sisters exploited their students and orphan inmates by having them sew for private customers, thereby undercutting small businesses. Some of the parents of children schooled by the sisters were among those who demanded that the asylum be burned down. It was burned and sacked, and the Sisters driven away. See Ullman 1968, 212–13.

16. Gabriel y Galán 1945, 713–15.

¿Quién es que os ha lanzado,
humanos ángeles,
en medio del estruendo
de los combates, donde los hombres
luchan y se destrozan
como leones?

¿Quién os manda a vosotras,
pobres mujeres,
a cerrar los ojos
de los que mueren,
y a ser las madres
de los que lejos de ellas
vierten su sangre?

¿Quién os lleva a la cumbre
del heroismo?
¿Quién os da fortaleza
para el martirio?
¿Quién os obliga
a inmolar por la ajena
la propia vida?

Lo sé, santas mujeres:
vuestro heroismo
es el de los amantes
hijos de Cristo.
¡No hay quien lo niegue!
¡La caridad cristiana
todo lo puede!

17. Barton 1898, 521. The reference to Armenia alludes to the slaughter of Armenians by Turks in 1895. Clara Barton worked to alleviate the suffering of the civilian population during that massacre, work that helped her later in Cuba when she ministered to the *reconcentrados*. For more information on Barton in Cuba, see Gardner 1954. See the appendix for a selection from *Del cautiverio,* by Manuel Ciges Aparicio, which presents a graphic description of a group of *reconcentrados* visited by him in 1896.

18. See Sales de Bohigas 1974, 209–19, for a discussion of the economic and social consequences of the *quinta* from the War of Independence up to and including the period

of the Cuban insurrections. She refers to literary works that dealt with the conscription, from Fernán Caballero to Gervasio Amat.

19. For this key event in the history of free speech in the 1890s, see contemporary coverage in *El Nuevo Régimen* (founded in 1891 by the republican federalist Pi y Margall) from September 1895 to February 1896, when Odón was restored to his post. For Odón's account of this period see Buen 2003, 62–65. As one of Spain's most indefatigable advocates of freethinking, Odón was often allied with other activist freethinkers, one of whom, Ángeles López de Ayala, is represented in the appendix. See Buen 2003, 71, for mention of a trip Odón arranged to a congress of freethinkers in Rome with Belén Sárraga, López de Ayala, and other atheists to celebrate the anniversary of the arrival in Rome on September 20, 1870, of Italian troops and the end of papal temporal rule. The appendix presents an extract from Odón's brief essay on women and science.

20. Ferrer Benimeli 1989, 56. The authors cited here have written two of the most relevant works on Masonry in Spain during the period in question: Ferrer Benimeli 1994 and, for women in Masonry, Morte 1989. See also the article by Ángeles López de Ayala published in the freethinking weekly *La Conciencia Libre* included in the appendix.

21. See Rodríguez González 1989, which contains a summary of the various stances taken by the Madrid press during the war, including a racist component found even in the articles written by the ostensibly liberal Luis Morote for *El Liberal*. For a presentation of press opinion on the Melilla campaign, nearly unanimous in urging punishment for the *rifeños* and the defense of the national honor, see Núñez Florencio 1900, 115–45.

22. Sixteen years later the Spanish government again sent troops to Morocco. In the bloody protests that followed in Barcelona and the surrounding towns, two thousand workers in Tarrasa on July 21, 1909, supported a resolution that combined anticlerical animus with complaints about conscription. Because of its relevance to the events of the 1890s, I quote it here in full:

Considering the fact that war is a fatal consequence of the capitalist system of production;

Considering also, the fact that under the present Spanish system, only workers go to fight the war which the bourgeoisie declare: The Assembly protests energetically:

1. Against the action of the Spanish Government in Morocco;

2. Against the proceedings of certain ladies of the aristocracy who insult the suffering of the reservists, of their wives and children, giving them medals and scapularies [*sic*] instead of providing them with the means of sustenance which is wrenched from them by the removal of the head of the family;

3. Against sending to war citizens useful to production and in general indifferent to the triumph of the Cross over the Half Moon, when they could form regiments of priests and monks who, besides being directly interested in the triumph of the Catholic religion, have no family nor home, nor are they of any service to the nation; and

4. Against the attitude of the republican deputies who have not taken advantage of their parliamentary immunity in order to take their place at the head of the masses in the protest against the war:

And it demands that the working class concentrate all its forces in the event that it should become necessary to declare a general strike in order to force the government to respect the right of Moroccans to preserve intact the independence of their nation. (Ullman 1968, 147–48)

## 2. Women and Violent Political Actions

Epigraph: Michel 1976, 127. "Si la reaction eût eu autant d'ennemis parmi les femmes qu'elle en avait parmi les hommes, Versailles eût éprouvé plus de peine; c'est une justice à rendre à nos amis, qu'ils sont plus que nous accessibles à une foule de pitiés; la femme, cette prétendue faible de coeur, sait plus que l'homme dire: Il le faut! Elle se sent déchirer jusqu'aux entrailles, mais elle reste impassible. Sans haine, sans colére, sans pitié pour elle-méme ni pour les autres, il le *faut,* que le coeur saigne ou non.

Ainsi furent les femmes de La Commune."

It is noteworthy that just as Galdós's essentialist assessment of women's nature fits them for the horrors of combat, so Michel's view of women's inherent capacity to do what has to be done gives them an advantage over men in bloody confrontations.

1. See Lida 1972, 268–69, for a list of books, pamphlets, and theatrical productions on the Paris Commune that appeared in Spain from 1871 to 1886. See also Termes 1965; and Ollivier 1971.

2. Quoted in Fagoaga de Bartolomé 1985, 60.

3. For a useful summary of the concurring opinions of Spanish scholars of feminism who have studied the marginalization of women by anarchists, socialists and communists, during the last third of the nineteenth century, see Palacio Lis 1992, 16–17.

4. See Núñez Florencio 1983, 193; Fernández Almagro 1969, 276–77; Esenwein 1989, 189–204; and Bookchin 1998, 109–10.

5. See Serrano 1987, 138–39. Rafael Pérez de la Dehesa (1968) attributes the reduction of the death sentences to five and the absolution for lack of incriminating evidence of sixty persons (who were nonetheless exiled) to the efforts of three newspapers: *El Socialista, El Nuevo Régimen,* and *El País* (691).

6. As for anarchist women's use of the press, *La Revista Blanca* (Madrid) published many articles by female anarchists on a variety of topics such as Soledad Gustavo's "El anarquismo y la mujer" (July 1, 1900), and "Concepto de la anarquía" (December 1, 1902) and Emma Goldman's "¿Qué es anarquismo?" (November 15, 1901). See Ortiz 2001, 73nn59, 60, 62.

7. Serrano summarizes the socialist and anarchist positions on anti-*quinta* propaganda and demonstrations, which in his view were unorganized and inadequate, in Serrano 1982, 271.

## 3. The 1896 Women's Demonstrations against Conscription

*Epigraph:* Campoamor 2006. "Respecto a la serie de afirmaciones que se han hecho esta tarde contra el voto de la mujer, he de decir, con toda la consideración necesaria, que no están apoyadas en la realidad. Tomemos al azar algunas de ellas. ¿Que cuándo las mujeres se han levantado para protestar de la Guerra en Marruecos? Primero: ¿y por qué no los hombres? Segundo: ¿Quién protestó y se levantó en Zaragoza cuando la Guerra de Cuba más que las mujeres? [...] ¡Las mujeres! ¿Cómo puede decirse que cuando las mujeres den señales de vida por la República se les concederá como premio el derecho a votar? ¿Es que no han luchado las mujeres por la República?"

1. The preceding text of this paragraph and the one before it is taken nearly intact from my 2001 book, O'Connor 2001, 66–67.

2. Lola Iturbe (1974, 31) writes that Sárraga was still coediting *La Conciencia Libre* in Córdoba in 1902. She participated in the 1933 elections, heading the list of federal candidates for Málaga. After the Civil War she went into exile in Mexico. Information on Sárraga is drawn in part from www.consejomujer.es/100mujeres-1etapa.html (accessed July 20, 2005). Lola Iturbe figures in the documentary featuring interviews with anarchist women filmed in 1986 by Lisa Berger and Carol Mazer, ... *de toda la vida* (New York: Cinema Guild), which also includes an interview with Federica Montseny, Soledad Gustavo's daughter; the film may be borrowed from the University of Vermont Library.

3. See Suñer 1938 for a later interpretation of Spain betrayed on the level of higher education, in particular by Jews, Marxists, and Masons, beginning with the founders and supporters of the Institución Libre de Enseñanza (1876).

## 4. Institutions That Shaped Women's Lives

*Epigraph:* "Carlota: Nos quieren los hombres apartadas de la política para que no reformemos sus inicuas leyes. Para ellos la libertad y el mundo; para nosotras la resignación y la obediencia. Mas no me quejo aún tanto de los hombres cuanto de las mujeres mismas. Mujer es mi madre, y es déspota para mí como no lo sería tal vez mi padre si viviera.

Julia: Libres nos hizo la naturaleza; esclavas la religion y las leyes. Ríome de los que dicen que nos emancipó el cristianismo."

1. See Scanlon 1976, 30–50, for the history and significance of the Asociación de la Enseñanza de la Mujer. Botrel 1982 provides detailed information on the control exerted by the Catholic Church in tandem with the state over all aspects of Spanish life; see also Montero García 1988. Education, the press, and the efforts of socialists and anarchists to change the system are discussed in Ortiz 2001. For key texts on education in nineteenth-century Spain, see Jagoe, Blanco, and Enríquez de Salamanca 1998, 147–217.

2. Ullman 1968 has many references to women's role in the uprising. See, e.g., 390n17, on the importance of women in organizing the general strike that sparked the uprising; 391n34, on the role of women in general; 186, for members of the women's organizations that suggested the burning of convents; 215, for a description of two women

who fought in the streets; and 232–33, for information on the backgrounds of some of the women who participated in the revolt.

3. Paloma Castañeda (1994) writes that when Carmen de Burgos joined the staff of the *Diario Universal* in 1903 and went out into the streets to gather material for her reports, she became the first woman reporter in Spain (27, 35).

## 5. Women's Voices

*Epigraph:* From "Crónica general," a regular column written by José Fernández Bremón, *La Ilustración Española y Americana* (Madrid), April 8, 1898. Bremón claimed to represent public opinion in snatches of dialogue such as this one. "—Qué dicen los soldados? / —¿Y los jóvenes? / —¿Y los viejos? / —¿Y las madres? / —Ya no tienen lágrimas: han derramado tantas que tienen seca el alma, y sólo sienten ira. La ola sube; la paciencia está agotada; se va cristalizando algo grande en la conciencia pública. ¿Qué va a suceder? Estará el Gobierno al unísono con ese sentimiento?" (198).

1. For a bibliography on these demonstrations, as well as Web sites to consult, see Herrera i Pujol and Lecha Adán 2003.

2. Fariñas Hernández 2005. *El Nuevo Herald* published several articles on the Ladies in White in 2004: "Insólita marcha de las Damas de Blanco en Cuba" on March 19, and "Oficialistas hostigan a esposas de disidentes," "Acto de repudio contra las esposas de los disidentes presos" and "Las Damas de blanco retan a la prensa oficialista" on March 21.

3. See Viñao Frago 1990, 584; and O'Connor 1995, 24–28, for a discussion of literacy in the 1890s.

4. See, e.g., Alberto Pla y Rubio's *De la guerra* and Manuel Picolo y López's *Adiós,* published in *La Ilustracion Española y Americana* in 1897 and 1898, respectively. These images are reproduced in O'Connor 2001, 42–43.

5. See O'Connor 2001, 130–39, for a discussion of *¡Quince bajas!* (reprinted in full in Spanish), as well as other relevant plays and zarzuelas.

6. See Sales de Bohigas 1974, 216–19. In Sales de Bohigas 1968, 274, the author wrote: "Popular discontent about the system of commutation was fanned by official admissions that the chances of survival in overseas campaigning were only 50:50. The system really amounted to 'poner precio a la sangre española, vender a pública subasta la vida de los ciudadanos' (putting a price on Spanish blood, selling citizens' lives at public auction). When the cry was raised in 1891, 'No one should go unless the rich go,' the Spanish parliament's response was to grant a bastard form of universal suffrage. In 1909, after tragic events which had begun as a demonstration against the embarkation of poor reservists (their families taking part), the Parliament finally moved toward making universal service compulsory by law. But the new law [passed in 1912] permitted men drafted for service in Africa to provide substitutes, while they themselves need then serve only in garrisons at home or in ministry offices. This partial commutation in Spain was ended only in the 1920s, *after* the last colonial wars."

# Conclusion

*Epigraph:* García Nieto 1975, 242. "Hay que tener presente también que, aunque en momentos determinados hubo censura, no obstante, el periodismo de 1895 a 1910 se rigió por las leyes de imprenta que concedían a todo español 'el derecho a emitir libremente sus ideas y opiniones, ya de palabra, ya por escrito valiéndose de la imprenta o de otro procedimiento semejante, sin sujeción a la censura previa.'" García Nieto quotes from the constitution of 1896 and refers the reader to the Press Laws of January 7, 1879, and July 26, 1882.

1. In May 1896 Antonio Cánovas was the head of government, and Mateo Práxedes Sagasta was the president of the Council of Ministers. Since exemption from service overseas through payment of two thousand pesetas was legal according to article 172 of the law of *reclutamiento y reemplazo del ejército* of August 21, 1896, Sagasta could in good conscience respond—as he did in November 1897 to a delegation from the National Committee of the Socialist Party, which "demanded compliance with article 3 of the Constitution, which imposes on all citizens the obligation of defending the national territory" (que se cumpla el artículo 3.0 de la Constitución del Estado, que impone a todos los ciudadanos la obligación de defender el territorio nacional)—that he (now head of state), along with the other members of the cabinet, was quite disposed to comply with the law (Hernández Sandoica and Mancebo 1978, 370–71).

2. The estimated number of anarchist papers is derived from the listing of workers' newspapers in Arbeloa 1970. This listing does not include the free-thought or Masonic papers for which women like Sárraga, Soledad Gustavo, López de Ayala, and others also wrote.

3. Lily Litvak (1981, 240–41) writes that anarchist works were widely distributed and read because they were cheap and easily available. For example, Claramunt's sixteen-page pamphlet *La mujer* (see the appendix) was distributed gratis (82).

4. See the discussion of commonly accepted racial attitudes regarding blacks in O'Connor 2001, 52–57.

5. For a study of investigations into the nature of women in this period, see Russett 1991. Russett identifies the contemporary scientific practices that made specious and fallacious judgments about women possible and credible to the public.

# Works Cited

## Newspapers and Periodicals

*La Conciencia Libre* (Valencia), 1896
*El Correo* (Madrid), 1896
*El Corsario* (La Coruña), 1896
*La España Moderna* (Madrid), 1891
*El Español* (Madrid), 1899
*El Globo* (Madrid), 1896
*La Ilustración Artística* (Barcelona), 1889, 1895–96
*La Ilustración Española y Americana* (Madrid), 1897–98
*La Ilustración Ibérica* (Madrid), 1894–95
*El Imparcial* (Madrid), 1894–98
*El Liberal* (Madrid), 1892–94
*La Lucha de Clases* (Bilbao), 1896
*Los Lunes de El Imparcial* (Madrid), 1893, 1896
*New York Times*, 1896
*El Nuevo Herald* (Miami), 2004
*El Nuevo Régimen* (Madrid), 1891, 1895–96, 1900
*El País* (Madrid), 2005
*La Política de España en Filipinas* (Madrid), 1896
*El Pueblo* (Valencia), 1896–97
*La Revista Blanca* (Madrid), 1900–1902
*El Socialista* (Madrid), 1896–97

## Books and Articles

Acuña, Rosario de. 1893. *La voz de la patria.* Madrid: R. Velasco.
———. 1989. *Rosario de Acuña: Rienzi el Tribuno / El Padre Juan (Teatro).* Edited by
   María del Carmen Simón Palmer. Madrid: Castalia.
Álvarez Angulo, Tomás. 1962. *Memorias de un hombre sin importancia (1878–1961).*
   Prologue by Dr. Carlos Blanco Soler. Madrid: Aguilar.

Álvarez Estévez, Rolando. 1976. *La "reeducación" de la mujer cubana en la colonia: La Casa de Recogidas.* Havana: Editorial de Ciencias Sociales.

Álvarez Junco, José. 1971. *La Comuna en España.* Madrid: Siglo Veintiuno.

Anderson, F. M., ed. 1908. *The Constitutions and Other Select Documents Illustrative of the History of France, 1789–1907.* 2nd ed. Minneapolis: Wilson.

Arbeloa, Victor Manuel. 1970. "La prensa obrera en España (1869–1899)." *Revista de Trabajo* 30:117–19.

Arenal, Concepción. 1942. *Cuadros de la guerra.* Buenos Aires: Editorial Nova. (Orig. pub. 1883.)

Balfour, Sebastian. 1997. *The End of the Spanish Empire, 1898–1923.* Oxford: Clarendon.

Barton, Clara. 1898. *The Red Cross: A History of this Remarkable International Movement in the Interest of Humanity.* Washington, DC: American National Red Cross.

Blasco Ibáñez, Vicente. 1978. *Artículos contra la guerra en Cuba.* Edited with a prologue by J. L. León Roca. Valencia: León Roca.

Blasco Ijazo, José. 1947. *Historia de la prensa zaragozana (1683–1947).* Zaragoza: Talleres Editoriales "El Noticiero."

Bonsal, Stephen. 1897. *The Real Condition of Cuba Today.* New York: Harper.

Bookchin, Murray. 1998. *The Spanish Anarchists: The Heroic Years, 1868–1936.* Edinburgh, Scotland: AK Press.

Botrel, Jean-François. 1982. "La iglesia católica y los medios de comunicación impresos en España de 1847 a 1917: Doctrina y prácticas." In *Metodología de la historia de la prensa española,* edited by Bernard Barrère et al., 119–73. Madrid: Siglo Veintiuno.

Brenan, Gerald. 1962. *The Spanish Labyrinth: An Account of the Social and Political Background of the Civil War.* New York: Cambridge University Press.

Buen, Odón de. 1892. "La mujer ante la ciencia." Prologue to *La mujer en el cristianismo,* by Cristóbal Litrán. Barcelona: La Academia.

———. 2003. *Mis memorias: Zuera, 1863–Toulouse, 1939.* Transcribed from the original manuscript by María del Carmen del Buen López de Heredia. Zaragoza: Institución "Fernando el Católico."

Burgos, Carmen de. 1927. *La mujer moderna y sus derechos.* Valencia: Editorial Sempere.

Cambronero, Carlos. 1891. "Malasaña y su hija." *La España Moderna* 3, no. 32:5–14.

Campoamor, Clara. 1939. *El pensamiento vivo de Concepción Arenal.* Buenos Aires: Editorial Losada.

———. 2006. "Discurso ante las Cortes el 1 de octubre de 1931." www.ciudad demujeres.com/mujeres/Política/CampoamorClara.htm.#Discurso (accessed July 20).

Canal, Jordi. 2000. *El carlismo: Dos siglos de contrarrevolución en España*. Madrid: Alianza Editorial.

Canel, Eva. 1897. *Albúm de la trocha: Breve reseña de una excursión feliz desde Cienfuegos a San Fernando, recurriendo la línea militar por cuatro periodistas*. Havana: "La Universal" de Ruiz y hermano.

Carr, Raymond. 1982. *Spain, 1808–1939*. Oxford: Clarendon.

Castañeda, Paloma. 1994. *Carmen de Burgos "Columbine."* Madrid: Horas y Horas.

Castelar, Emilio. 1874. *Miscelánea de historia, de religión, de arte y de política*. Madrid: A. de San Martín.

———. 1908. *Correspondencia de Emilio Castelar, 1868–1898*. Madrid: "Sucesores de Rivadeneyra."

Caudet, Francisco. 1999. Introduction to *Paz en la guerra*. Madrid: Cátedra.

Chambers, John Whitelay, II. 1991. "Conscription." In *Reader's Companion to American History*, edited by Eric Foner and John A. Garrity, 216–19. Boston: Houghton Mifflin.

Ciges Aparicio, Manuel. 1930. *Del cautiverio*. 2nd ed. Madrid: Editorial España.

———. 1986. *Del cuartel y de la guerra: El libro de la crueldad*. Edited by Cecilio Alonso. Alicante: Instituto de Estudios "Juan Gil-Albert."

Claramunt, Teresa. 1905. *La mujer: Consideraciones generales sobre su estado ante las prerrogativas del hombre*. Mahón: n.p.

Clemente, Josep Carles. 1982. *Las guerras carlistas*. Barcelona: Península.

Clodfelter, Micheal. 2001. *Warfare and Armed Conflicts: A Statistical Reference to Casualty and Other Figures, 1500–2000*. Jefferson, NC: McFarland.

Coello, Carlos. 1875. *La monja alférez*. A historical zarzuela in three acts and in verse. With music by Maestro Marqués and a prologue by José Gómez de Arteche, distinguished member of the Academia de la Historia. First performed in the Teatro Jovellanos on November 24, 1875. Madrid: Fortanet.

Eichner, Carolyn J. 2004. *Surmounting the Barricades: Women in the Paris Commune*. Bloomington: Indiana University Press.

Elshtain, Jean Bethke. 1982. "Women as Mirror and as Other: Toward a Theory of Women, War, and Feminism." *Humanities in Society* 5, no. 2:29–44.

———. 1987. *Women and War*. New York: Basic Books.

Erauso, Catalina de. 1829. *Historia de la monja Alférez doña Catalina de Erauso escrita por ella misma*. Edited by Joaquín María de Ferrer. Paris: Julio Didot.

———. 1992. *Vida i sucesos de la monja Alférez: Autobiografía atribuída a doña Catalina de Erauso*. Edited by Rima Vallbona. Tempe: Center for Latin American Studies, Arizona State University.

Esenwein, George Richard. 1989. *Anarchist Ideology and the Working-Class Movement in Spain, 1868–1898*. Berkeley and Los Angeles: University of California Press.

Fagoaga de Bartolomé, Concha. 1985. *La voz y el voto de las mujeres, 1877–1931.* Barcelona: Icaria.

Fariñas Hernández, Guillermo. 2005. "Las damas de blanco." Cubanet_d@topica. email-publisher.com. January 7.

Feijóo Gómez, Albino. 1996. *Quintas y protesta social en el siglo XIX.* Madrid: Ministerio de Defensa.

Fernández Almagro, Melchor. 1969. *Historia política de la España contemporánea, 1885–1897.* Vol. 2. Madrid: Alianza.

Fernández Bastarreche, Fernando. 1988. "The Spanish Military from the Age of Disasters to the Civil War." In *Armed Forces in Spain Past and Present,* edited by Rafael Bañón Martínez and Thomas M. Barker, 213–47. New York: Columbia University Press.

Ferrer, Ada. 1998. "Rustic Men, Civilized Nation: Race, Culture, and Contention on the Eve of Cuban Independence." *Hispanic American Historical Review* 78, no. 4:663–86.

Ferrer Benimeli, José A. 1989. "Evolución histórica de la masonería española." In *Exposición La Masonería Española, 1728–1939,* exhibition catalog, edited by José A. Ferrer Benimeli et al., 39–62. Alicante-Valencia: Instituto de Cultura "Juan Gil-Albert."

———. 1994. *La Masonería.* Madrid.

Fiestas, José María, ed. 1984. *Guía del Museo del Ejército.* Madrid: Torreangulo Arte Gráfico.

Fuller, Margaret. 1980. *Women in the Nineteenth Century.* Facsimile of the 1845 edition with an introduction by Madeleine B. Stern and textual apparatus by Joel Myerson. Columbia: University of South Carolina Press.

Gabriel y Galán, José María. 1945. *Obras completas.* Madrid: Aguilar.

García Nieto, María del Carmen. 1975. "La prensa diaria de Barcelona de 1895 a 1910." In *Prensa y sociedad en España (1820–1936),* edited by M. Tuñón de Lara, A. Elorza, and M. Pérez Ledesma, 241–70. Madrid: Cuadernos para el diálogo Edicusa.

Gardner, Arthur. 1954. *Clara Barton, Protector of the Cuban "Reconcentrados."* Havana: Sociedad Colombista Panamericana.

Goldman, Emma. 1931. *Living My Life.* Vol. 1. New York: Knopf.

———. 1987. *Social Significance of the Modern Drama.* Introduction by Harry G. Carlson, preface by Erika Munk. New York: Applause Theatre Books. (Orig. pub. 1914.)

Goldstein, Joshua S. 2001. *War and Gender: How Gender Shapes the War System and Vice Versa.* Cambridge: Cambridge University Press.

Gómez de Arteche, José. 1875. Prologue to *La monja alférez*, by Carlos Coello. Madrid: Fortanet.

Green, Nathan C. 1896. *Story of Spain and Cuba.* Baltimore: International News and Book Co.

Gullickson, Gay L. 1996. *Unruly Women of Paris: Images of the Commune.* Ithaca, NY: Cornell University Press.

Hernández Sandoica, Elena, and María Fernanda Mancebo. 1978. "Higiene y sociedad en la Guerra de Cuba (1895–1898): Notas sobre soldados y proletarios." *Estudios de Historia Social* 5–6:361–84.

Herrera i Pujol, Laia, and Marc Lecha Adán. 2003. "Las madres de la resistencia: El discurs maternalista de las Madres de la Plaza de Mayo, una expresión de pacifisme." In *Las mujeres y las guerras: El papel de las mujeres en las guerras de la Edad Antigua a la Contemporánea*, edited by Mary Nash and Susanna Tavera, 301–5. Barcelona: Icaria.

Higonnet, Margaret Randolph, Jane Jenson, Sonya Michel, and Margaret Collins Weite, eds. 1987. *Behind the Lines: Gender and the Two World Wars.* New Haven, CT: Yale University Press.

Hijos de J. Espesa, eds. *Enciclopedia universal ilustrada europea-americana.* 1929. Madrid: Espasa-Calpe.

Holt, Edgar. 1967. *The Carlist Wars in Spain.* London: Putnam.

Iturbe, Lola. 1974. *La mujer en la lucha social y en la Guerra Civil de España.* Mexico: Mexicanos Unidos.

Jagoe, Catherine, Alda Blanco, and Cristina Enríquez de Salamanca, eds. 1998. *La mujer en los discursos de género: Textos y contextos en el siglo XIX.* Barcelona: Icaria.

Jaques y Aguado, Federico, and Manuel Fernández Caballero. 1887. *Cuba Libre.* Madrid: José Rodríguez.

Kaplan, Temma. 1987. "Women and Spanish Anarchism." In *Becoming Visible: Women in European History,* edited by Renate Bridenthal, Claudia Koontz, and Susan Stuard, 402–21. 2nd ed. Boston: Houghton Mifflin.

Langle Rubio, Emilio. 1911. *La mujer en el derecho penal.* Madrid: Hijos de Reus.

"Ley de reclutamiento y reemplazo del ejército de 11 de julio de 1885 modificada por la de agosto de 1896." 1896. *Boletín de Legislación y Jurisprudencia* 102 (November): 765–820.

Lida, Clara E. 1972. *Anarquismo y revolución en la España del XIX.* Madrid: Siglo Veintiuno.

Litvak, Lily. 1981. *Musa libertaria: Arte, literatura y vida cultural del anarquismo español (1880–1913).* Barcelona: Antoni Bosch.

López Gómez, Jesús. 1896. *Cuba*. Madrid: R. Velasco.

MacKinnon, Catharine. 2006. *Are Women Human? And Other International Dialogues*. Cambridge, MA: Harvard University Press, Belknap Press.

Martínez Cuadrado, Miguel. 1969. *Elecciones y partidos políticos en España (1868–1931)*. Madrid: Taurus.

Martínez Sanz, Isidro. 1896. *Familia y patria*. 2nd ed. Madrid: Evaristo Odriózola.

Medina, Isagani R. 1995. "Gregoria Montoya y Patricio: Wife of Cirilo Ayson, Later of Pedro Cacpal." In *Women in the Philippine Revolution*, edited by Rafaelita Hilario Soriano, 88–89. Quezon City: Printon.

Medio, Dolores. 1966. *Isabel II de España*. Madrid: Editorial Sucesores de Rivadeneyra.

Merrim, Stephanie. 1999. *Early Modern Women's Writing and Sor Juana Inés de la Cruz*. Nashville: Vanderbilt University Press.

Michel, Louise. 1976. *Mémoires*. Paris: François Maspero. (Orig. pub. 1886.)

Millán, Pascual. 1899. *¡Quince bajas!* Madrid: El Enano.

Miret Magdalena, Enrique, and Javier Sádaba. 1998. *El catecismo de nuestros padres*. Barcelona: Plaza & Janés.

Montero García, F. 1988. "Propaganda católica y educación popular en la España de la Restauración." In *École et église en Espagne et en Amerique Latine: Aspects idéologiques et institutionnels; actes du colloque de Tours (4–6 décembre 1987)*, introduction by Jean-René Aymes, Éve-Marie Fell, and Jean-Louis Guereña, 264–79. Tours: Publications de l'Université de Tours.

Morte, Libertad. 1989. "La mujer y la masonería." In *Exposición La Masonería Española, 1728–1939*, exhibition catalog, edited by José A. Ferrer Benimeli et al., 99–104. Alicante-Valencia: Instituto de Cultura "Juan Gil-Albert."

Nash, Mary. 1983. *Mujer, familia y trabajo en España (1875–1936)*. Barcelona: Anthropos.

Nelken, Margarita. 1975. *La condición social de la mujer en España*. Prologue by María Aurelia Capmany. Madrid: CVS.

Nuez González, Ada de la, ed. 1978. *Mujeres en revolución*. Havana: Editorial de Ciencias Sociales.

Núñez Florencio, Rafael. 1983. *El terrorismo anarquista, 1888–1909*. Madrid: Siglo Veintiuno.

———. 1990. *Militarismo y antimilitarismo en España (1888–1906)*. Prologue by Manuel Espadas Burgos. Madrid: Consejo Superior de Investigaciones Científicas.

O'Connor, D. J. 1995. *Crime at El Escorial: The 1892 Child Murder, the Press, and the Jury*. San Francisco: International Scholars Press.

———. 2001. *Representations of the Cuban and Philippine Insurrections on the Spanish Stage, 1887–1898.* Tempe, AZ: Bilingual Press.

Ollivier, Albert. 1971. *La comuna.* Translated by Patricio de Azcárate Diaz. Madrid: Alianza Editorial.

Ortiz, David, Jr. 2001. "Redefining Public Education: Contestation, the Press, and Education in Regency Spain, 1885–1902." *Journal of Social History* 35, no. 1:73–95.

Oyarzun, Román. 1969. *Historia del Carlismo.* Madrid: Alianza Editorial.

Palacio Lis, Irene. 1992. *Mujer, trabajo y educación (Valencia, 1874–1931).* Valencia: Universitat de Valencia, Departamento de Educación Comparada e Historia de la Educación.

Palacio Valdés, Armando. 1946. *Marta y María.* Buenos Aires: Espasa-Calpe. (Orig. pub. 1881.)

Pardo Bazán, Emilia. 1896. "Dos de Mayo." *La Ilustración Artística,* April 27.

———. 1956. *La Tribuna.* In *Emilia Pardo Bazán: Obras completas,* edited by Federico Carlos Saínz de Robles, 2:113–225. Madrid: Aguilar.

Payne, Stanley G. 1967. *Politics and the Military in Modern Spain.* Stanford, CA: Stanford University Press.

Pérez de la Dehesa, Rafael. 1968. "Los escritores españoles ante el proceso de Montjuich." In *Actas del Tercer Congreso de Hispanistas, 1968,* 685–94. Mexico City: El Colegio de México.

Pérez Galdós, Benito. 1950. *El equipaje del rey José.* In *Obras completas,* edited by Federico Carlos Saínz de Robles, 1:1183–1270. 3rd ed. Madrid: Aguilar.

———. 1953. *Zaragoza.* Madrid: Hernando. (Orig. pub. 1874.)

———. 1958a. *La campaña del Maestrazgo.* In *Obras completas,* edited by Federico Carlos Saínz de Robles, 2:773–871. 4th ed. Madrid: Aguilar.

———. 1958b. *Vergara.* In *Obras completas,* edited by Federico Carlos Saínz de Robles, 2:963–1068. 4th ed. Madrid: Aguilar.

———. 1958c. *Zumalacárregui.* In *Obras completas,* edited by Federico Carlos Saínz de Robles, 2:321–418. 4th ed. Madrid: Aguilar.

Perillán de Buxo, Eloy, and Pedro Marquina. 1871. *El sitio de París.* Madrid: José Rodríguez.

Perrot, Michelle. 1987. "The New Eve and the Old Adam: Changes in French Women's Condition at the Turn of the Century." In *Behind the Lines: Gender and the Two World Wars,* edited by Margaret Randolph Higonnet, Jane Jenson, Sonya Michel, and Margaret Collins Weite, 51–60. New Haven, CT: Yale University Press.

Pick, Daniel. 1989. *Faces of Degeneration: A European Disorder, c. 1848–c. 1918.* New York: Cambridge University Press.

Pierats, José. 1990. *Anarchists in the Spanish Revolution, Part 2: From the Beginnings to the First Great Struggles*. London: Freedom Press.

Posada, Adolfo. 1899. *Feminismo*. Madrid: F. Fe.

Prados-Torreira, Teresa. 2005. *Mambisas: Rebel Women in Nineteenth-Century Cuba*. Gainesville: University of Florida Press.

Puell de la Villa, Fernando. 1996. *El soldado desconocido: De la leva a la "mili" (1700–1912)*. Madrid: Editorial Biblioteca Nueva.

Ramón y Cajal, Santiago. 1939. *Mi infancia y juventud*. Buenos Aires: Espasa Calpe.

Reverter Delmas, Emilio. 1897. *Filipinas por España: Narración episódica de la rebelión en el Archipiélago Filipino*. Vol. 2. Barcelona: Centro Editorial de Alberto Martín.

Revista de Tribunales. 1896. *Ley de reclutamiento y reemplazo del ejército de 11 de julio de 1885, modificada por la de 21 de agosto de 1896, con el reglamento para su ejecución y el de declaración de exenciones del servicio del ejército y la marina de 23 de diciembre de 1896, anotada y concordada por la redacción de la Revista de Tribunales*. Madrid: Centro Editorial de Góngora.

Reyes Churchill, Bernardita. 1995. "Agueda Kahabagan y Iniquinto." In *Women in the Philippine Revolution*, edited by Rafaelita Hilario Soriano, 66. Quezon City: Printon.

Rochat, Giorgio. 1973. "L'esercito italiano negli ultimi cento anni." In *Storia d'Italia*, vol. 5, edited by Ruggiero Romano and Corrado Vivanti, tome 2, pp. 1869–1902. Turin: G. Einaudi.

Rodríguez González, Agustín. 1989. "El conflicto de Melilla en 1893." *Hispania* (Madrid) 178:240–44.

Romeo Mateo, María Cruz. 2000. "Juana María de la Vega, condesa de Espoz y Mina (1805–1872): Por amor al esposo, por amor a la patria." In *Liberales, agitadores y conspiradore*, edited by Isabel Burdiel and Manuel Pérez Ledesma, 209–38. Madrid: Espasa-Calpe.

Russett, Cynthia Eagle. 1991. *Sexual Science: The Victorian Construction of Womanhood*. Cambridge, MA: Harvard University Press.

Sales de Bohigas, Nuria. 1968. "Some Opinions on Exemption from Military Service in Nineteenth-Century Europe." *Contemporary Studies in Society and History* 10, no. 3:261–89.

———. 1974. *Sobre esclavos, reclutas y mercaderes de quintos*. Barcelona: Ariel.

Scanlon, Geraldine M. 1976. *La polémica del feminismo en la España contemporánea (1868–1974)*. Madrid: Siglo Veintiuno.

Schwartz, Robert M. 2004. Review of David M. Hopkin, *Soldier and Peasant in French Popular Culture, 1766–1870*, by David M. Hopkin. www.H-France.net (accessed March 4).

Scott, Joan. 1987. "Re-writing History." In *Behind the Lines: Gender and the Two World Wars*, edited by Margaret Randolph Higonnet, Jane Jenson, Sonya Michel, and Margaret Collins Weite, 21–30. New Haven, CT: Yale University Press.

Sempau, Ramón. 1900. *Los victimarios*. Barcelona: García Manet.

Serrano, Carlos. 1982. "Prófugos y desertores en la Guerra de Cuba." *Estudios de Historia Social* 22–23:253–78.

———. 1984. *El final del imperio: España, 1895–1898*. Madrid: Siglo Veintiuno.

———. 1987. *Le tour du peuple: Crise nationale, mouvements populaires et populisme en Espagne (1890–1910)*. Madrid: Bibliotheque de la Casa de Velázquez.

Simón Palmer, María del Carmen. 1992. "Biografía de Eva Canel (1857–1932)." In *Estudios sobre escritoras hispánicas en honor de Georgina Sabat-Rivers*, edited by Lou Charnon-Deutsch, 294–304. Madrid: Castalia.

Soriano, Rafaelita Hilario. 1995a. "Josefa Rizal y Alonso." In *Women in the Philippine Revolution*, edited by Rafaelita Hilario Soriano, 100–101. Quezon City: Printon.

———, ed. 1995b. *Women in the Philippine Revolution*. Quezon City: Printon.

Stoner, Lynne K. 1991. *From the House to the Streets: The Cuban Woman's Movement for Legal Reform, 1898–1940*. Durham, NC: Duke University Press.

Suñer, Enrique. 1938. *Los intelectuales y la tragedia española*. San Sebastián: Editorial Española.

Termes, Josep. 1965. *El movimiento obrero en España: La primera internacional (1864–1881)*. Prologue by Carlos Seco Serrano. Barcelona: Publicaciones de la Cátedra de Historia General de España.

———. 1986. "El anarquismo en España: Un siglo de historia (1840–1939)." In *El anarquismo en Alicante (1868–1945)*, 11–26. Alicante: Instituto de Estudios "Juan Gil-Albert."

Thurman, Judith. 1999. *Secrets of the Flesh: A Life of Colette*. New York: Ballantine.

Tiongson, Nicanor G. 2004. *The Women of Malolos*. Quezon City: Ateneo de Manila University Press.

Tombs, Robert. 1999. *The Paris Commune, 1871*. Harlow, Essex, UK: Wesley Longman.

Tone, John Lawrence. 1999. "Spanish Women in the Resistance to Napoleon, 1808–1814." In *Constructing Spanish Womanhood: Female Identity in Modern Spain*, edited by Victoria Loreé Enders and Pamela Beth Radcliff, 259–82. Albany: SUNY Press.

Ullman, Joan Connelly. 1968. *The Tragic Week: A study of anticlericalism in Spain, 1875–1912*. Cambridge, MA: Harvard University Press.

Unamuno, Miguel de. 1999. *Paz en la guerra*. Ed. Francisco Caudet. Madrid: Cátedra.

Urruela, María Cristina. 2001. "Becoming 'Angelic': María Pilar Sinués and the Woman Question." In *Recovering Spain's Feminist Tradition*, edited by Lisa Vollendorf, 160–75. New York: Modern Language Association of America.

Vega Martínez, Juana María de la, Condesa de Espoz y Mina, with María Lafitte, Condesa de Campo Alange. *Memorias*. Madrid: Tebas, 1977.

Velasco, Sherry. 2000. *The Lieutenant Nun: Transgenderism, Lesbian Desire, and Catalina de Erauso*. Austin: University of Texas Press.

Viñao Frago, Antonio. 1990. "History of Literacy in Spain: Evolution, Traits, and Questions." *History of Education Quarterly* 30:573–99.

Walker, D. J. 2006. "The *Monja-Alférez Rediviva* in the Service of General Weyler: Eva Canel in Cuba." *Wadagabei: A Journal of the Caribbean and Its Diasporas* 9, no. 2:4–29.

Weber, Eugen. 1986. *France, Fin de Siècle*. Cambridge, MA: Harvard University Press.

Whittam, John. 1977. *The Politics of the Italian Army, 1861–1918*. London: Croom Helm; Hamden, CT: Archon Books.

Zamora y Caballero, Eduardo. 1895. "Los soldados de la Independencia: Las mujeres." *La Ilustración Artística*, March 4, 180.

# Index